Sinéad
  So pleased you
were able to make it!
Yours was a face I
returned to many times!
    Love

Dr. Mary Helen Hensley

Promised

Book Hub Publishing
An Independent Publishing House
Galway, Ireland
www.bookhub4u.ie

First Published in Ireland in 2009 by
Book Hub Publishing
www.bookhub4u.ie

2nd edition

Visit our author's interview on www.bookhub4u.ie

Dr. Mary Helen Hensley asserts the moral right to be identified as the author of this work.

ISBN: 978-0-9562801-0-7

Cover Design by Noel Cassidy, Book Hub 4u

Jacket Photo by Dr. Mary Helen Hensley

This book is available direct mail order from www.bookhub4u.ie

Acknowledgements

My first and most heartfelt thanks go to the Universe and all of the amazing beings that reside within its loving embrace. I owe the story of my life and how it has been blessed, to the unwavering support of those that dwell in the infinite realms. I have been touched by their constant presence and am forever grateful for the small role they have allowed me to play as a facilitator of healing the minds, bodies and spirits of some of my fellow human beings.

To my family, thank you so much for choosing me as a member of your clan. My mother and father have provided the most joyous experience for one in search of truth and love. Their willingness to promote not oppress, to advise not judge and to love unconditionally has made me who I am today. To the extended cast-my brothers and sister and each of their spouses; I could not have asked for a better supporting crew. Each member of my family, from Grandparents, aunts and uncles, nieces and nephews and cousins galore, has contributed countless opportunities for my soul to grow.

Everyone I have ever encountered has been a teacher in my life. To those who actually had the challenge of formally teaching me, I thank you for your tenacity. The Martinsville Public School System, Carlisle School, Coker College, Patrick Henry Community College, Trident Technical College, and Greenville Technical College all provided me with a background that allowed me to flourish as a student of life. My special thanks go to Dr.'s Tom and Betty Gelardi for their vision and fulfilment of the dream that became Sherman College of Straight Chiropractic, the special place where I learned how to think outside of the proverbial box. I am eternally grateful to all who taught me there.

To all whom have been mentioned in this book by name, regardless of whether the names have been changed to respect your privacy, you have played an enormous role in my journey and I thank you for each and every lesson you have taught me. There have been no negatives, only mirrors that have reflected the best opportunity to get a lesson through my thick little skull. There are no ex's or former friends, because I treasure the time I had with you, no matter how brief, and value and understand the contribution that each of you has made to my life. I give my deepest and sincerest thanks to you all. I thank your soul, Jase, for knowing that I could write this book better a second time, and for helping me to bring our daughters to life.

I thank all of those who have supported me in so many different ways while I wrote this book. To the staff of the Radisson SAS Hotel in Athlone, your comfortable lobby became my writer's den and not once did I have to ask for a pot of tea- it was always on the table before the laptop was even turned on. To Maureen, for listening to me read the same stories over and over and over again, always smiling and telling me what worked and what didn't. I wouldn't even 'Be' if it weren't for you. My thanks go to Irene, Madame Butterfly, for a list that would make a book in, and of, itself. I also want to thank Suzi for her eagle eyes, gentle and eloquent feedback, and genuine interest in the success of this project. Thanks to Jacq for your deep sense of knowing and intuitive guidance and to Emu for the laughter and always telling me I could do this. To Kate, a real live Earth Angel, your love and support are priceless. To Mick, your daily injection of humour renews my spirit. I especially appreciate all of my friends who suffered through reading the rough drafts and giving most helpful feedback. I will forever be grateful for the suggestions made by Neal Donald Walsch as to the direction I should take in telling this story. Huge thanks to Stevie for encouraging me to "get off the road" and take this to the public. Thanks to Gerry for the hours and hours of typing and to Tanya for weathering the storm. My most heartfelt thanks to Lew for lifetimes of love and support; our work has simply picked up where it left off. Thanks to Jubal Tiner and Tara McDonald-Tiner of Coachwrite for their expertise in editing. T, I thank you for you're amazing contributions and suggestions, as well. I love your spirit. To Niall, my new friend, agent and publisher all rolled in to one-what can I say, dude? You rock!! The Bookhub Publishing House fell straight from the heavens and I look forward to a long and lasting friendship. Thanks for making that happen, Emer. To all of my friends, and particularly those near and dear to me in Ireland, your support over the last ten years has been invaluable.

But most of all, I want to thank my beautiful, extraordinary and gifted little girls, Jemma Skye and Jada Pacifica, who challenge me to be a better person, reminding me every single day why I chose this life path. Their depth of spiritual understanding and compassion towards all forms of life never ceases to amaze me. I am forever, your grateful student.

Chapter Layout

"To one who has faith,

No explanation is necessary.

To one without faith,

No explanation is possible."

St. Thomas Aquinas
(1225-1274)

Prologue

Imagine two unborn babies in their mother's womb. One is a believer that life lies ahead and the other, a disbeliever, believes only death is ahead. They are arguing together in the mother's womb.

The believer says, "Nature has been at work on us for nine months and nature isn't crazy. It means something. Something is coming of this. We're not just going to die."

"What are you talking about?" says the disbeliever. "There's no such thing as living outside of the matrix of this womb. We'll be cut off from all nutrition. Of course we're going to die!"

"No!" says the believer. "Things have been going on here for the last nine months that have prophetic meaning. I believe in the wisdom of nature."

"Well," continues the disbeliever, "describe to me exactly what you think is going to happen."

And with that, the believing baby is stuck. He can't imagine anything like sunshine, breathing or eating; running, jumping or playing. So the argument ends with the disbeliever seeming to have won.

- Unknown

Chapter 1
Accidents Happen

"You're one lucky little lady." The voice seemed to float in from beside me with a deep and soothing southern drawl. "Are you feeling strong enough to tell me what happened?" My nose burned with the smell of disinfectant, and every square inch of my body ached as if I had been trampled by a herd of wild elephants. I opened my eyes and tried to focus on the man standing next to me. As my sight adjusted to the harshly lit room, I realised that I was in a hospital, and the man that was speaking to me was not a doctor, but a policeman. There were nurses walking in and out from behind a curtain, constantly checking monitors, smiling, but saying nothing. I could hear a woman's voice requesting assistance in the E.R. over a loudspeaker.

I looked over at the officer, careful not to make any sudden movements, because it felt as if my head would split in two if I did. In a raspy voice that sounded as if I hadn't had a drop of water in days, I said,

"Hey, I know you. You were at the accident."

"That's right," he replied, with a slightly puzzled look on his face. "Can you remember any details that might help me figure out how all of this happened?"

I swallowed and grimaced with pain, not realising that I had fractured a bone in my neck and that the rest of my spine was now shaped like a backward letter C. I thought back to earlier in the afternoon, when I had set out on a short drive to town, and suddenly blurted out,

"You should talk to my friend from college. She was only a few cars behind me when it happened and saw the whole thing! Did you find the piece of paper on the front seat of the car? A lady put it there, and it had her name and number on it, but then she ran away. There was a guy in some kind of uniform and he turned the engine off. Surely he saw something!"

The officer became visibly uncomfortable and confused.

"Young lady," he said. "How do you know about the lady who put her phone number in the car?"

"I saw her, of course."

"And just how did you know that your friend was at the scene of the accident?"

"I saw her, too," I replied, starting to get a little agitated.

With a tone much less confident than when our conversation had begun, he said,

"Miss, there is *no way* you could have seen any of that happen! Your friend…the lady with the phone number…the man in uniform. All of those things were going on while you were still unconscious and pinned in the car."

It was at that moment, the penny dropped.

I struggled to pull myself up so that I could look my inquisitor in the eye. What I was about to tell him was going to change me in ways that I could never imagine. I immediately became emotional as I proceeded to tell him what had really happened that afternoon. He listened carefully as I described exactly how the accident had taken place and the unusual circumstances that surrounded it. He stared at me with his mouth partially open, his brow wrinkling as he listened on in amazement and confusion. It all seemed *so* clear to me, but obviously he was very disturbed by the uncanny way I was able to describe the incident. When I had finished, he asked no more questions. In fact, he didn't say another word and quietly left the room.

As I sat on the hospital bed, I looked around at my sterile surroundings and reflected on what I had told the policeman, but more so, things I *hadn't* told him. The day had started out like any other, but what had transpired that evening was nothing short of miraculous, and until now, *no one has ever heard it in its entirety.*

Regarding Immortality

An old man of eighty-one, dressed in dirty overalls and worn-out work boots, got into his car to run a few errands in the afternoon. He drove down Highway 17, one of Charleston, South Carolina's, busiest motorways, and proceeded towards his destination. No one will ever know if he simply didn't see the red light, or if he sped up in an attempt to make it through the intersection before the oncoming traffic entered. His speed would indicate the latter, and his collision with a young couple earlier in the year suggests his deteriorating driving skills and slow reaction time should have taken him off the road permanently. We never met face to face, but this man's life was now forever entangled with mine. He shot through the traffic light and broadsided my car, hurling me into oncoming traffic. The impending impact literally knocked me out of my body.

My first lesson in death was that no matter how we die; in an accident, a murder, or even from an illness; we can exit the body just prior to its actual demise, *if we choose to do so.*

The day was unusually warm, even for the South. It was the 14th of December, 1991, and I was on my way to a Christmas party. Dressed in a Santa Claus tee-shirt and bright red Bermuda shorts, I had just left my apartment and reached the end of my road, when I was about to become the newest member of that old statistic that states, "most accidents occur within two miles of home." Waiting for my light to turn green, I had no idea that the crossroads before me was to be the metaphorical and metaphysical crossroads of my life.

As I drove through the intersection, I looked into the far lane of traffic and could see a car racing towards me. I quickly realised that the driver had absolutely no intention of stopping at the red light. I didn't have time to brake or swerve, and due to the fact that I was about to take a direct hit to the driver's side door, known as a t-bone impact, I knew I didn't stand a chance.

Time ground to a halt as I felt my body brace for the collision. *Then a funny thing happened.* I became consciously aware that not only was this accident *waiting* to happen, it was waiting for me to make a *decision.* I was consumed with a clarity I am still unable to adequately describe. I had the distinct choice of remaining in my body, experiencing the impact with all senses intact, or I could simply exit, allowing the remainder of the scene to unfold without having to feel the imminent sensation of having my body crushed.

It all seemed very natural, and it felt as if I had all the time in the world to make this decision – time truly can stand still. Its deceptive illusion is *so obvious* when faced with death. I was overwhelmed with a certainty that I had "been there and done that" so many times before, and I sensed I had nothing to gain from experiencing this impact *inside* my body. It was this choice that has shaped the rest of my life. Because this time, unlike the countless times before, *I remembered dying.* Call it evolution of the spirit or an old soul finally figuring it all out. At that moment, I became engulfed by the peace that passes all understanding. I was comfortable with the familiarity of it all as I recognized that I was not about to become a victim of death, but an active participant in my own passing.

Time resumed at an explosive rate as I catapulted upward and out of my body, moving instantly from participant to spectator. I watched the old man's car smash into mine, and I could hear the festive jingle bell necklace I wore around my neck banging out an eerie tune at the instant I saw my head smash into the driver's side window. The sound of bending steel echoed as I watched the driver's seat fold in half beneath my body. I looked on with peculiar and detached interest as blood began to soak through my clothes. The glass had shattered and flown up my shorts, cutting my most personal areas and embedding into my bare legs. The safety belt had pinned me to the back of my seat, as if my battered frame was hanging in suspended animation. As the momentum slowed, the car finally came to rest in the middle of the highway, stopping six lanes of traffic in its tracks.

Now out of my body, I noticed that a friend from college had been only a few cars behind me at the same stop light and observed her horror as she recognized the mangled body that was trapped inside the now crushed Toyota Corolla. It was then it occurred to me as strange – that I had just *witnessed* this accident. A shocked state of awareness set in as I took note that I was effortlessly floating, looking down at the body that had taken me through twenty-one years of life, and it did not bother me that I was no longer inside it. I quickly adjusted to the absolute freedom of being unencumbered by a physical body and watched as the rest of the scene continued below.

A lady, who was either in a rush to be somewhere else, or too afraid to get involved at the time, ran over to the car, placing her name and phone number on the front seat of the passenger side. A man in uniform reached in, turned the ignition off and frantically looked to see if he could pull me out. He soon realised that the entire left side of my body was pinned between what was left of the seat and the bashed-in driver's side door. He tried to keep onlookers from getting in the way. People were rapidly beginning to congregate, some attempting to offer a helping hand, but most just trying to catch a glimpse of the wreckage and the unfortunate person it belonged to.

As I began to gather my wits, I comprehended that I was transitioning from life into death, and one of my greatest childhood fears was instantaneously dissolved. I had always had a terrible dread that when we die, we cease to exist. Poof! Gone! No memory or identity, just nothing. It was a ridiculous fear for me to have, since I had been exposed to so many extraordinary paranormal experiences earlier in my life. Nonetheless, it was still a deep-seated anxiety that periodically gripped me in my youth, no matter how many times I had seen proof of life after death. I was overjoyed to realise that I knew exactly who I was, with all memories intact, but with a complete lack of concern for my body and the end of the life I had been living only moments before.

I know people have described near-death experiences with the "tunnel of light". I did see the light, but the trip through the tunnel must have been so fast that I actually missed it. I will, however, never forget the *sound* that accompanied me on this journey. It was the most bizarre buzzing noise, unlike any hum I had ever heard. It was present as I watched what happened on the ground; however, a most beautiful drone replaced it as I landed in a magnificent bright light. One second I was hovering above my car, watching the spectacle that was my own accident, then, in a flash, I was somewhere else. Somewhere so amazing that my human mind and limited vocabulary could never articulate its awe-inspiring beauty.

Without delay, I became conscious of two "beings," illuminated by the most stunning backdrop of light I have ever seen. The colours weren't from our world, as I have never seen such translucence in a rainbow or vibrant shades in any work of art. I was surrounded by a mixture of a distant relative of magenta with a shimmering, pearly sheen. The atmosphere seemed to breathe this unusual colour with a palpable texture; I could feel it all around me. These two "beings" appeared to be a part of these colours, yet seemed to step from the palate, taking on a solid and recognizable human form. They were wearing what resembled flowing gowns, but the caramel coloured material from which the gowns were made looked to be a part of them, as opposed to separate pieces of clothing.

14

They greeted me with a love and joy so pure; it was as if I felt myself melt right into them. For a moment, I became *one* with them. I had temporarily become that extraordinary colour of light and could feel it coursing through my soul, cleansing me and welcoming me home. It was perfectly clear that the spirits before me were not friends or family from the life I had just left. They were guardians that had spanned millennia with me, watching and guiding lovingly from this place that was becoming more familiar as each second passed.

The stories were true! These were my guides, my spiritual watchdogs. *They really exist!* They were there to assist me in my transition from living in the physical world to life on the spiritual plane. I was now becoming fully aware of how I had known these beings, sharing in the excitement of this reunion. I soon realised that we were not speaking in the manner I had been accustomed to in my earthly existence. We were sharing from our hearts, soul to soul, in a universal language that knew no bounds or limitations. There were no words spoken; only thoughts and feelings that filled my spirit with lucidity that far surpassed that of any dialogue I had ever partaken in on Earth.

I was flooded with the memories of how it all began; an odyssey of adventures as my lifetimes unfurled before me. The backdrop of colour that greeted me on my arrival was now like a cinema screen, surrounding me 360 degrees and in multiple dimensions. In a single instant, it all became crystal clear. I was ready to examine the story of my life. With the interest of an actress critiquing her own performance it was li ke watching a film with your best friends.

My spiritual cheerleaders wrapped me in their love and proceeded to guide me, step by step, through twenty-one years on earth as Mary Helen Hensley; the marvellous, the mediocre and the dreadfully disappointing bits of my colourful young life.

How startling it was to see how tiny gestures had snowballed into life-changing moments for those who had witnessed them, and how heartbreaking it was to see the same effect with thoughtless acts and unkind words. Still, I watched, taking mental notes as to where I had been excellent and taken on soul-inspiring lessons about the importance of kindness and compassion in *all* situations. I became painfully aware of how, along the course of history, the phrase "judge not lest ye be judged," had been invariably altered, losing its most vital point – that no one great deity judges us in the end; it is *we* who must judge our own performances. A daunting prospect when watching your life play out in front of you, aware of the contents of each scene, unable to change them, and *knowing* what's coming next.

In that all-loving space, I understood that it was me, myself, to whom I must be accountable.

Much to the disappointment of my friends in the Bible belt of the United States, there was no fire and brimstone; no wrath of a vengeful God. *Only the hushed solitude of a place so beautiful, it hurts to remember.*

While looking back at my life, I was experiencing humankind's most difficult challenge – to sit with one's self. The experience was despairing as well as euphoric, but ultimately it was love revealed in its highest form, which no person should fear. Remaining ever mindful that every second really does count, that in the midst of all of the chaos, joy and pain, a.k.a. *life*, we are never disconnected or more than a "passing" away from home.

To adequately and fully describe all that went on during that journey back to the Source of Life would take volumes. To be honest, many details as to the inner workings of life's greatest secrets were hidden behind a veil of forgetfulness which those in spirit must have felt was necessary to conceal, so those that return may live a productive life. To pine away for the splendour and love of that extraordinary place would be to throw away the precious, short time we have in this world.

One of the benefits, or burdens, of remembering your death, is a feeling of tremendous responsibility to always strive to do the right thing. To treat people with anything less than kindness, fairness and respect, carries a heavy price tag when you are able to remember your own death. The intensity of emotion while witnessing your life story is one that I will never be able to translate appropriately. Remembering beyond the veil carries an indescribable sense of *knowing* that isn't always that easy to live up to when dealing with others, especially those who don't remember what lies ahead. It gives new meaning to rising to the occasion, turning the other cheek, doing unto others, and all of the other clichés to which we have become numb. I think of the quote: "A hero is someone who is excellent when *no one* is looking." But guess what, heroes; someone *is* looking and it is *you*.

Of the many things that I can remember, I think it is important to state that reincarnation is a *fact*. It's not some dreamy fantasy those who are afraid to die sooth themselves with in order to quell their fears or lessen their apprehension. I will emphatically profess, without any reservation, *we have lived before*. We have lived here, and in many other places, just as we will continue to do so until such time as the great unknown becomes fully revealed. Earth is one of many options for growth and expansion, and just like going to school, we come here and reincarnate here, until we are finished here. We don't jump in and out of "Earth school" – we work our way through until we feel that we have exhausted all offered and can move on. I had experiences of this knowledge as a child, and now I stood face-to-face with the reality that life really does go on.

17

It was the relaxed and very familiar way the guardians guided me through the journey of my life that made this all so evident. While watching the stories of my life, I was building on the knowledge and information gathered from previous lifetimes. It all became obvious during this process, which also made it easy to disengage from any feelings of blame, resentment, or anger towards missed opportunities of accomplishment in the life I had just left. The prospect of moving up and onward in a different body, with a different set of circumstances, was patiently waiting around the corner.

I discovered that we are like actors in a guild that tend to incarnate together, taking on various roles in different lifetimes. In this life, I am playing the part of daughter to my mother and father, the sibling of my two brothers and one sister, and currently, I have the role of the mother of two beautiful little girls. I have played the girlfriend, the wife, divorcee, and now, single mother. I have been the student as well as the teacher, and a doctor, turned metaphysician and author. In my next life, any of these people may appear as a parent, a partner, a good friend, or even an aggravator. This is why all of us have had the experience where we felt as if we knew someone we have never met before, or taken an instant liking or disliking to another person for seemingly no reason at all. As for soul mates, I discovered that we have many.

What we need to remember, as we get caught up in the romantic notions of finding our one true soul mate, is that we may have decided long ago to experience life with several of our soul mates, as friends, family or lovers. We play our roles in one another's lives, loosely following a script that allows the freedom of improvisation at each actor's discretion. This is the stuff that being human is made of. It is what makes life so worth living. While you might be following your lines word for word, your co-stars may choose to deviate from the script, throwing you completely off track and into a situation that creates even more opportunities for growth and expansion of the soul.

The term "soul group" has been used to describe these players, and is an appropriate description for how it all works. Members of a soul group tend to incarnate together, teaching or learning a similar set of lessons in conjunction with the other members of the group. They support one another through many journeys, and certain themes have a tendency to appear consistently, as each member strives to reach a new level of spiritual awareness. It is a most amazing approach to living and one that will never allow the human race to grow tired of its self.

For example, a soul yearning to learn compassion may return to this world as a dastardly character, ruthless and without conscience. He may find a soul mate in his child, a cherished and long awaited heir, who is then taken away, killed by cruel and tragic circumstances. The soul that died knew prior to incarnation that its time on Earth was limited. Its mission was to provide an arena for its companion soul to experience tremendous feelings of grief and loss, possibly resulting in a better understanding of compassion.

Another soul wishing to learn lessons in devotion may find itself married to the most disloyal of spouses, not because this soul is inherently unfaithful, but because it is playing the part of the infidel, so that the soul on the receiving end of this painful relationship might embrace the value of commitment.

The combinations are endless, and members of the same soul group have a complete understanding of the roles they will play before the curtain even opens. All roles, whether we understand or embrace their value, are equally important, and by the same token, divine in the eyes of our creator. It changes one's entire perspective and begs the question *"Is it actually possible for another person to harm us?"*

For those who have lost loved ones to violence or acts of malice, it is nearly impossible to comprehend. But in the grand scheme, each and every spirit is fully aware of who they are to become; aware that perceptions may be that they are anything *but* an all loving spiritual being. But no matter what appearances may seem each life is a crucial component in the expansion of the heart of humanity, while furthering its own evolution.

I remembered exactly why I had chosen to incarnate into my family. Its specific value system and any idiosyncrasies were all custom-ordered in my personal development and any advancement my spirit had set out to achieve. My father's dedication to spiritual and physical discipline, paired with my mother's overwhelming capacity to see the good in everything, were a combination that I requested in order to obtain the background necessary to accomplish my work in adulthood. The respect that I had for my brothers and sister without sharing a deep emotional closeness was also part of the plan. I had chosen to become a member of a family unit that had allowed me to grow and develop with an independence that was never overshadowed by any one sibling's influence. One brother and my sister provided complete stability and "normality". My oldest brother inspired a sense of adventure and mystery. They were equally important pieces of the puzzle of my life. We had been born so far apart that I spent the vast majority of my time on my own, developing my personality traits and building close friendships outside the family.

My siblings were meant to be an easy source of love and friendship rather than a battleground for life lessons this time around. I had chosen a different curriculum this lifetime that had primarily to do with my parent's belief system, the teachings of Christianity, and integrating that influence into my own personal convictions – the ones that had been formed from my individual experiences. It all made so much sense now: why I had spent so much time on my own with my parents as a pre-teen and young adult. I had more to gain from what I was to discover when being weaned from my mother and father than I did by waging war or developing extremely close relationships with my brothers and sister. My guardians had rekindled my understanding of just how vital the choosing of one's family is to laying the foundation of who we are to become in the future.

I was overcome with a new zest for living and a tremendous feeling of recommitment to my life on Earth. My spiritual teachers, the Guardians, knew before I breathed this thought…I was going to go back. I recognised that I just wasn't finished yet. We do have that choice, and as I learned that day, there are many opportunities to leave this life, *if we choose to take them*. These are what I call *portals of exit*. They are the near misses – we've all had them – close calls that could have been *the big one*, the lucky break; the miraculous recovery by the grace of God, the time when "someone was definitely looking out for me." I learned that our higher selves are well aware of these portals; it is our own souls that determine how and when we use them. I had just squeezed through a portal to study my performance rather than letting it pass me by. I was now preparing to shove myself back through it, with a new vision from a place I now remember as home.

The spirits impressed upon me that there is not one life set in stone, with a concrete beginning and an unchangeable end. That would be incongruent with the way the rest of the universe operates. Free will, it's been called in the past, but it's more like
Thy will be done… on Earth, as it is in Heaven.

I had always thought that *thy* meant God's will, when in actuality, it means our own free will and what we chose to do with it. Portals of exit give us the chance to be the authors of our own stories, not puppets on a string, doing the bidding of an unwavering or disinterested Master. We can write and rewrite our stories as we go along, with the guidance of our spiritual companions and departed loved ones. It is the most amazing part of the grand plan. We have been given the tools to experience ourselves in life for as long or as short as we choose, with as much happiness and health, or as much

21

pain and suffering as we see fit in order to learn the lessons of growth and development that this earthly school has to offer. Thankfully, I retained that memory; it is the keystone on which I have built the foundation of my entire life.

I had been given a wonderful gift. The chance to live on, make changes and begin a new direction in life, complete with fresh memories of where I had come from; *The place where all of us have come from.* I had also been given specific impressions of how my life would change when I returned. *Things would definitely not be the same.* I would go back into my body, with access to different gifts and abilities that I had not been privy to before the accident. The bar had been raised, and so much more was going to be expected of me, if I chose to follow this path. I knew that this course of action was not going to be easy; however, with this endowment also came a promise; constant guidance and support, if only I would open my heart and allow myself to receive.

With no tearful goodbyes – in fact with no farewells at all – I heard a deafening, whooshing noise; it sounded so harsh compared to the environment I had just been in. Pain and terror were the next things I felt as I was sucked back into my body, which was now out of the wreckage and lying on the road. I have no memory of how I got there. I know I had regained consciousness before the ambulance arrived. Knowing me, I probably demanded to show that I was okay and had convinced somebody to let me stand on my own. I vaguely recall speaking to and then seeing my boyfriend's sister, first by phone, then when she arrived at the scene just before I left for the hospital. There were brief moments of lucidity, as if I had only been in a minor "fender bender" in the car. However I got there, I was now in shock and in a heap on the hard pavement before being strapped to a board, immobilised and placed in an ambulance.

A lady was leaning over me and stroking my hair, attempting to soothe me as I sobbed, trying to piece together what in the world had just happened. She kept saying over and over that there was no way they were going to let me die, most likely because I kept crying and talking about dying. She thought that I was fearful that I might actually be passing away, when little did she know, I was babbling about the fact that I had *already* died. I *knew* that I was going to make it, but at that stage, I couldn't have told her or anyone else *why*. My encounter with that beautiful place, those colours, my Guardians, now seemed like a distant dream as I faded in and out of consciousness, on the way to the emergency room.

Unbelievably, I was released from the hospital just a short time later, never scanned or x-rayed, riddled with a host of unidentified and very serious injuries. It used to boggle my mind as to how this could have happened. My car was hit at an estimated 60-70 mph, yet somehow I slipped through the cracks, only to discover how badly I had been injured weeks, months, and years later. I have since developed a greater understanding as to why this was all part of the plan. Each wound brought me closer to the new path that had been laid out before me. Divine timing was most certainly at work. As far as the medics in the hospital were concerned, they had patched me up as best as they could, and it was time for me to go and face up to the emotional trauma of this crash on my own. My boyfriend, Ben, took me home when I was released, where I spent the night in shock and bewilderment, but most of all in the horrific pain of a physical body that now felt like a two-ton weight, compared to the spiritual body that had just taken me to another world and back again.

For the first time in my colourful medical history, I downplayed my story when I called my parents. No gut wrenching tales of twisted steel and smashed glass, no stories of blood and broken

23

ribs; hearing loss or head injuries. Not a word was mentioned about where I had actually been, who I had met there, or the fact that I had been so lovingly reminded of the reason I came into this life in the first place. I simply told them that I had been in a little accident. No big deal. They were so far away, it was night time, and the news that I had died and come back was a little much for anyone to stomach just before bed.

It was a long time before I told them what really happened, and I never really gave the full story to my boyfriend or his family. I just didn't think they were ready. As I now realise, it was me who wasn't able to share. I played the scene over and over in my mind trying to figure out if this all could have been the product of smashing my head through the driver's side window. Easy enough to explain my life review and the "beings of light" as hallucinations, but I would have imagined that my "delusions" and all of the information I was exposed to would have been in some way congruent with my current beliefs, or at the very least, in line with the way in which I had been raised to believe things were. I also simply couldn't explain away the fact that I had seen the collision take place, as well as the people who came to my aid, all with a bird's eye view of my unconscious body. I would discover soon enough that this most certainly had not been due to any sort of delirium.

Ready or not, Pandora's Box had burst open. The young girl that had always experienced the peculiar dreams and visions – she who communed freely with spirits as a child – was now about to understand why her entire life had been leading to this day, this serendipitous "accident", this glimpse of another world, and most of all, the incredible new course that life was about to take.

Chapter 2

When you were a tiny baby, you were pure joy and love. You knew how important you were; you felt you were the centre of the universe. You had such courage, you asked for what you wanted, and you expressed all of your feelings openly. You knew you were perfect. And that is the truth of your being. All the rest is nonsense and can be unlearned. - **Louise L. Hay**

The Promise

On February 23, 1969, I slid comfortably into my place as the youngest of four in the Hensley clan. By all accounts, the day was unforgettable. I was born in a heavy snowstorm in the Shenandoah Valley of Virginia. My parents didn't have snow tyres on their car, so had to solicit the help of a friend with chains on his tyres to get Mom to the hospital in time. The rest, as they say, is history. It was exactly ten years to the day after my sister Beth had made the journey. I always thought it was so cool that we shared the same special day; however, through the eyes of a ten year old, I'm sure she felt differently about sharing the limelight with her new baby sister. I arrived safely with all parts intact, despite the grim prognosis my folks had been subjected to over the previous nine months.

My mother had been diagnosed with Rubella in her first trimester of pregnancy, something no mother-to-be wants to hear, as it can be seriously damaging to a growing baby's health. Along with fears of possible blindness, hearing or limb loss, Mom was also slightly older than the average mother at the time. This was a point that I would so graciously bring up whenever I got into trouble as a child; blaming any poor behaviour on the fact that I was probably never right in the head because she was *so old* when she had me. While I'm sure opinions as to my being "normal" have varied over the years, I was as normal as any other healthy child and suffered no known side effects from my mom's illness, other than a peculiar gleam in my eye and a slightly twisted sense of humour.

For as long as I can remember, my Dad has told me that I was *promised*. I never really understood the relevance of this as a child, but it seems that he was *visited*, informed by divine inspiration, and assured that not only would I be born without complications from the German Measles, but that I was destined to live a very "special", unusual and lengthy life. The information he received during this celestial visit left him confident that my place in this world was secure and that I would always be assisted by spiritual intervention in my endeavours throughout life. Dad always described the feeling as overwhelming, and he knew with certainty that the promise that had been made was one that would be kept. I know that all parents have these wishes for their children, but there was something different, emphatic even, about the way he expressed this knowledge. He had faith, believed it to be so…and so it was.

I was always made to feel like a gift. I was forever being reminded that this sacred promise had been made and that nothing or no one could ever change this fact.

Daydream Believer

I have never been a great sleeper. From the cradle onward, two hours here, a catnap there, has always been standard fare for me. Most definitely an inherited trait from my father as my mother can, and has, slept through violent storms - including tornados. My mind seems to rev up rather than wind down at night. The hours of darkness have always been a strange, exciting time, full of anticipation as well as a bit of a foreboding feeling. I have always awakened in the morning with vivid memories of the previous night's dreams, which seem to "stick" with me throughout my day.

Throughout childhood, I regularly experienced the distinct feeling of leaving my sleeping body and taking flight, sometimes around my home or out into the neighbourhood. I also recall "visiting" people I knew, as well as those I had never met before, feeling their feelings and seeing their dreams. Often times I would awake with a clear picture of events that were about to take place. When I told my Mom about these experiences, she said that she too, had also remembered "flying" on many occasions while she slept. Standard dream material some would say, but these sojourns into the night were not the average. I was well aware from an early age that *something unusual was going on.*

Doc Clark

A man would appear in my dreams most nights from as early as I can remember. He would tell me stories by showing me images while I slept. From the time I was able to write, I used to love to put these stories on paper and then perform them as plays. I was always interested in topics that seemed a little too grown up for the average kid. I was in my element when I was put into the classroom of my second grade teacher, Miss Smith. Just recently, she recounted a story from my childhood to my mother, about how she had received a phone call from me one Saturday morning, heralding the news of the upcoming performance of a new play I had just written. It was about a doctor involved in the first expeditions to the North Pole – loosely based on fact – with the details having been filled in by my dreamtime companion. My controlling tendencies were already beginning to show, as I arrived in school on Monday and performed the one girl show, playing all characters, bar the dying patient, who had no lines. The beautiful, wonderful Miss Smith, as I always referred to her, not only allowed, but encouraged this unusual behaviour. No one ever knew where I really got these stories, but this dreamtime companion, *my grandfather*, never let me down.

27

There is only one photo of Dr. Garland Clark, holding his three month-old granddaughter, less than a year before his death in 1970. It was Easter, and the picture made it very clear that his body was exhausted and he wouldn't be around much longer. I never thought much about not knowing him in life, because he seemed to always be around at night when I was sleeping. The fact that I woke so often is what allowed me to become skilled at recalling what went on during those hours. I definitely attribute my interests in health and medicine to the "special appearances" he made throughout my childhood. The influence that this man was to have on me would take another twenty-something years to realise. It was to become a landmark discovery in my life.

A Day at the Beach

I had an unusual mental image that would occur on a regular basis any time my family would take a vacation near the water. Whenever we went to the beach, I always got a very distinct visual of driving down a road and seeing sand dunes ahead of us. I could envision driving onto the beach and seeing a number of small tents placed randomly around the sand, with people in old-fashioned bathing costumes emerging from these makeshift dressing rooms and playing on the beach.

At the time, I never understood that these "waking dreams" were somehow triggered by physically being in the location. I have now come to realise that these visions were glimpses into the past – some kind of collective universal memory. I knew that they weren't my own memories, but they certainly belonged to someone. They were like energetic impressions in my mind of what the area had actually looked like in years gone by. I often experienced this sensation, not only near the beach, but when visiting any new destination. It was like having a "mind movie" of the past and it always made me appreciate the places we visited, especially because both of my parents were history buffs. They were forever taking us to battlefields, colonial townships, war memorials, battleships and graveyards, all which held the energy of amazing historical events.

One summer in particular, my parents, my brother, Jonathan, and I took a trip to the beach. As was customary for our travels, no reservations had been made, and we always took a chance, hoping for the best when searching for somewhere to stay. It was Virginia Beach, and the region had been plagued with a severely eroding coastline. We had tried several spots before finally coming to rest at a hotel that was located directly on the beach. On the shore side of the hotel, there was a massive undertaking to pump sand onto the dwindling beach, and I was fascinated by the whole operation. I wasn't much older than four or five and had been duly warned not to go near the pipes that were blasting sand in front of the hotel and further up the beach. It was very late and we had spent most of the evening looking for somewhere to stay. As my parents unloaded the car, curiosity got the best of me despite numerous words of caution. I wandered down to the beach to see what was going on.

Unbeknownst to my parents, who were still trying to get our things into the hotel, I was gone in a flash! I had walked off in the wrong direction and was now perfectly lost, as children are so adept at doing. As soon as my folks realised I was missing, my father embarked on a frantic journey that to this day, he says, aged him twenty years.

I continued to walk, eventually coming upon two men that could only be described as hippies. It *was* the early seventies, and with their Doobie Brothers hairstyles and beach bum motifs, it looked as if I had landed in the middle of a really bad 70's sit-com. They were sitting around a small fire, with sleeping bags and a makeshift stove, talking and laughing. I remember a funny smell coming from the skinny

29

little cigarettes they were smoking. I walked straight up to them and in my innocence, asked if they knew where my mom and dad were. They were very kind and asked me what hotel we were in. I instantly offered up the name of one of the many hotels we had tried – of course, it was one that had no vacancy. Hand in hand, these two men walked me down the beach to the hotel I had told them, only to find that my parents were not there. Luckily, the hotel clerk remembered suggesting another place to stay to a man and his family and maybe if we checked there, we might find them.

My hippies and I turned the other way and walked back up the beach to our new destination. Several hours had now passed and I was having the time of my life! My parents, of course, were distracted with worry. We entered yet another hotel from the beach–side entrance and I remember my mother's face as she saw me cross the threshold with my new found friends. As there were no mobile phones at that time (they were as futuristic as compact discs or cable TV), there was no way to notify my father until he returned on his own. I was absolutely petrified of how angry he was going to be.

I had no regard in my young mind as to the drama I had caused over last few hours. My only concern was that I had disobeyed orders and would most certainly be punished. When he eventually returned, I saw my dad in tears for the first time in my life. He was livid, but mostly relieved as he lectured me as to the danger I had put myself in. The reason this story is so significant in my history is that my father went in to great detail as to *how I could have drowned* that night.

A Blast to the Past

As a great little swimmer, a Pisces by nature, I never had a fear of the water, only deep respect for and great pleasure from all it had to offer. As my father lectured on, his voice was reduced to a murmur and seemed to fade into the background as I spontaneously recalled a memory of having drowned before. I appeared to be staring off in space as my mind transported me to a place that to this day I can't name, but remembered as vividly as if I had been there the day before. Oddly enough, as I

re-experienced this part of my past, I was not afraid, nor did I equate the present night's experience with what it meant to drown. I had unexpectedly dredged up from my extensive biography, what drowning meant *to me*.

Getting lost on that beach did not come close to the feeling of standing outside of a temple of some sort, in a modestly embellished, full-length purple gown, watching fiery objects sail through the sky. I appeared to be in my early thirties. I distinctly recall looking across a field at the village that held my family home. I had been frantically working inside of the temple in some sort of preparation for the impending devastation. A global catastrophe had sparked off a massive tidal wave that quickly took me to my death. As I went under the colossal wall of water, I felt the fear and sadness of going through this alone, without being able to hold my children as they faced their imminent deaths. The only thing remotely similar to this memory and my current beach adventure was that this time around I *could* have, but *didn't* drown *and* I was separated from my family. I was lost in this unexpected flashback, the first of many to come, when Dad snapped me back to the present.

"Do you understand me, young lady?" was the next thing I heard.

Dad was still lecturing, not realising that I had just experienced my very first recollection of death in a former life. I knew enough to know that losing me for the night had been a little too traumatic to share this new insight with my parents. This experience was to be filed away and not spoken about until many years later, a habit that I had already begun to master.

Armageddon

I revisited the memory of drowning from a different perspective when I was in the fifth grade. It was a Wednesday afternoon. I know this, because I was at church where I spent every Wednesday afternoon and evening of my childhood. Hand bell practice, then Family Night dinner followed by choir practice was the normal routine from about age four until I graduated from high school. I remember this particular evening so well because I had spent the whole of the day waiting in fear for five o'clock to arrive. The talk around school had been that on *this* day, the planets were supposed to align in such a way that Earth was to see her last moment before exploding at around five that evening. There had been something mentioned in the papers and some reference on the news that had led us to believe that this Wednesday was to be our last, as our planet was ripped apart due to this unique stellar alignment. Real or not, the fear it conjured up in me was absolutely staggering.

I asked one of my teachers from school, who was also a member of our church, if this was truly the fate we were to meet. With complete calmness, Ms. Simpson held my hand and said she genuinely didn't think so. She then said that if it was going to happen, hadn't we been so lucky to have lived the time that we had? I will never forget that moment, because so often adults dismiss children and their fears. Ms. Simpson gave me her undivided attention, along with her real feelings about a situation that had me in the most panicked state that I had ever experienced. Her single act of interest and honesty was one that has inspired me to always listen to the concerns of young people, no matter how silly they may sound. I felt respected, and most of all heard, not brushed off because my worries were childish or stupid.

Needless to say, five o'clock came and went, but I remained on high alert for the rest of the night, just in case somebody had the time wrong. The overwhelming terror I was experiencing was heightened by flashbacks of that woman in the beautiful purple gown looking up into the sky as flaming asteroids, meteors or pieces of another planet streaked by, just before the giant wall of water took her to her death. I had not thought of this since I had been lost at Virginia Beach several years earlier. These feelings of sadness and fear were just so familiar to me, as my parents had not yet arrived at the church for dinner, and I thought that I might die without them by my side.

To this day, I have a disproportionate reaction to anything dealing with outer space, asteroids, comets, shooting stars, etc. I will not watch movies with this theme and if I happen to glance at a tabloid heading with anything to do with the subject, I immediately get a bit panicky. Spiritual development and a bit of maturity have allowed me to put these fears into perspective, but nonetheless, my heart still pounds a little harder when I see or hear about these celestial events. I do not believe that past lives necessarily dictate the person that we become, but I do know that our past lends itself to creating tendencies in our present, regardless of what our rational minds tell us to accept as truth.

Even the Smallest Acts of Kindness

When I was a child, I absolutely loved spending time with senior citizens. So much so, that as I look back now, I realise this affinity went well beyond what would be considered normal affections. If you were to visit the First Baptist Church in Martinsville, Virginia and ask any member of the congregation what they remember about little Mary Helen Hensley, I guarantee the response would be "She always loved the old people." Every week, as the congregation arrived for Wednesday Night supper, I made a point to go around and hug every old person before they sat down to eat. Even though my friends were off playing, I wanted each and every one of these dear ones to know that cared for them deeply.

Our children's choir would regularly visit the nursing home. We would walk up and down the hallways singing songs, and those who were able would stand at their doors or roll up in their wheelchairs. I remember wanting to set them free, like animals in a zoo or pet store, because they deserved to be loved and to grow old with their loved ones. At that age, I did not understand the reality of the situation. Some of these people had no one to look after them or needed care beyond the means available to their families. Still, I desperately wanted these elderly ones to feel worthwhile and to know that I respected their life experiences, even though I was a child.

This affinity for the aged was to impact my life in a way that I couldn't have imagined. There was a couple in our church that I was particularly fond of. The Burroughs had never had any children of their own, and I was always surrounded by their acts of financial generosity towards our church and community. I used to love to make things for them because I was very conscious of the fact that they had no "home made" items that only a child could create. I remember so well when Mr. Burroughs passed away because I can still hear Mrs. Burroughs telling me that she was certain that she would die of a broken heart. She did, only six months later, *my first understanding of how our emotional and physical states are so deeply entwined.*

Just after Mrs. Burroughs died, my father received a phone call from another member of our church who happened to be the head of one of our local Banks. Dad was asked to come down to the Bank and to bring me with him. We were asked if we had any idea why we were there and neither my father, nor I, could give an answer. The Bank administrator proceeded to read a piece of paper that said a lot of things that I didn't understand. He then recounted how much Mr. and Mrs. Burroughs had cared for me. Because I simply loved these people, they had left a considerable amount of money to be applied towards my College education. I will never forget the look on my Dad's face. It wasn't the look of joy that one would expect as a huge monetary burden had just been lifted, it was the look of absolute pride, as he experienced one of those moments that only a parent can understand, watching your child truly "get" one of life's biggest lessons.

A huge message was heard that day. While I had no concept as to how much this meant to my parents from a financial standpoint, I had learned that taking the time to show love and concern often meant more to people than I could have ever imagined. At the time, I was unconsciously just spending time with people that I loved. I have since learned the tremendous power of taking the time to simply show that you care. A gesture that costs me nothing more than a thought could potentially change the entire course of someone else's day or life, including my own.

Chapter 3

Think you that God cannot laugh? Do you imagine that God does not enjoy a good joke? It is your knowing that God is without humour? I tell you, God *invented* humour.

- **Neale Donald Walsch**

Is There a Doctor in the House?

The human body has always fascinated me. I was absolutely thrilled when I got my first Doctor's kit as a child. The little black bag contained a plastic stethoscope, a thermometer complete with elevated temperature reading and a blood pressure cuff that registered dangerously high numbers on its red paper dial. Every night, I would check Mom and Dad for any ailments that might have cropped up during the day. Dad always required a bandage around his head, and he would sit patiently and allow me to wrap him up like a mummy. I quickly realised that the longer I stayed in "Surgery," the later I got to stay up. I spent most nights massaging backs, pounding calves and performing minor surgery on bumps, lumps, cysts, and pimples. I would routinely prepare Dad for his ops by shaving his face with lotion and a butter knife. I often cupped my hands around my mother's knee and imagined filling it with "good energy." She had destroyed that knee while helping me climb out of a swimming pool when I was two, and I always felt so sorry for her when I saw the big surgical scar across her leg.

Along with my love of doctoring my folks came an obsession with my own infirmities. I was constantly talking about illnesses, real or imagined, that bordered on hypochondria. If the truth be known, I loved being sick. It's really quite bizarre when I think of it now. I loved going to the doctor; I couldn't wait to hear the explanation of

37

what was happening to my body, and I was utterly disgusted when I would get some average ailment like a sinus infection or the flu. I was delighted with each and every diagnosis of the standard childhood diseases. I proudly boasted when I received my *second* bout of Mumps (each side of my face had been infected individually) and considered myself very lucky to have contracted the dreaded Fifth disease, a distant relative of the measles. I was only too thrilled to back my brother, Jon, into a corner, waving my rash-covered arms in his horrified face!

I soon realised that *sickness equalled leverage and power*, an unfortunate preview of how I would manifest real illnesses to escape any number of stressful situations in the years to come.

One New Year's Eve, I was playing football with the children in the neighbourhood. I was seven going on seventeen when I ran deep to make a spectacular catch from my brother, the quarterback. I caught the pass but slipped on the grass and fell to the ground, smashing my chin into the ball. The only thing that kept my teeth from smacking together was my tongue. I bit straight through it and nearly severed it in two. It required a number of stitches and was good for almost a month's worth of sympathy, as well as a new pair of Hush Puppies shoes, my reward for being so brave. It was totally worth it because I had been begging for those shoes for months and only something as serious as biting off my tongue gave good enough reason for Mom to cave in and make the purchase! It has made for a lifetime of great stories, complete with an amazing scar for visual effect.

My love of ailments was a running joke in our family. Mom and Dad always went on a date every Saturday night as they still do, fifty-four years later. A phone number was always left in case of emergency. I don't think a single Saturday night was free from a phone call to the restaurant, in which I preceded my news with,

"Now don't you worry, but..."

One time I was sure my teeth were growing *up* through the roof of my mouth instead of *down*, and another time I was certain that my appendix was ready to burst. You can be sure that it was always something very serious, as well as very unique.

My sicknesses always seemed to worsen during the school year. It wasn't that I didn't like school, because I did. However, there was something at the time that meant much more to me than the academic world. I was a tremendous fan of old movies. These were the kind my parents would have seen in the theatres as they were growing up. I knew each and every star from Virginia Mayo and Maureen O'Hara to the Marx Brothers and the Three Stooges. I would dance around with Ginger Rogers and Fred Astaire, go West with "The Duke" and travel on hilarious adventures with Bob Hope and Danny Kay. I was mesmerised by Bing Crosby's voice and could watch Gene Kelly glide on air all day long. It was remarkable how my temperature would drop and I would suddenly feel better at one o'clock, just in time for the feature film. There were even times when I started my day at school but deteriorated just in time to be home for the afternoon line-up. It didn't happen often, as my folks wouldn't allow it – and there *really* were days that I wasn't well, but I cherished the days when I was lucky enough to spend the afternoon with my Hollywood heroes.

Money Talks

There was no such thing as spare time in my youth. If I wasn't in school or at church, I was out pounding the pavements trying to sell things. I was a whiz at pushing Girl Scout cookies, and I also had my own little business selling greeting cards. I had joined a kid's sales club that rewarded reaching sales targets with quirky items out of a catalogue that couldn't be bought in the shops. I was the only kid on the block that owned a genuine wristwatch radio. Never mind it was nearly the size of a normal radio with a wrist strap attached – no one else had one. I thought I was the coolest kid in town as I literally dragged my arm around, playing static-filled music everywhere I went.

I loved selling things, mostly because people always buy things from little children, so rejections were few and far between, boosting my already self-inflated confidence. I also loved making my own money. I found it satisfying, knowing that I had earned money myself, rather than being given an allowance, like most of my friends. While other kids were collecting money for chores that my parents considered family obligations, I began to develop a deep appreciation for the value of money. Instead of paying me to make my bed or to take out the garbage, Dad used to select books on positive thinking and health and pay me a "reader's fee" when I finished each one.

I worked my way through many phenomenal books throughout my teens. I hit the jackpot in more ways than one when I made it through Tony Robbins's life changing masterpiece, *Unlimited Power,* for a staggering *fifty dollars*. That was big, big money in those days. Dad had no idea that many years later, I would get to meet Tony and his wife at a seminar and express my gratitude for his inspiring words. Dad's methods instilled within me a great work ethic, as no one pays me now to do my housework, but I am paid every day for my knowledge about the mind, body and spirit.

Third Highest F in the Class

If I had to sum up the greatest qualities given to me by my parents in two words, those words would be *attitude* and *gratitude*. My father was, and still remains, a top notch disciplinarian. I mean this in the most positive sense of the word. I have yet to meet an individual as dedicated to a personal regimen of health and fitness as my father. His attitude towards the care and upkeep of both his mental faculties and physical body made no room for laziness or excuses, and is the reason that he still thrives today at eighty-two. His attitude towards his relationships with his wife and children saw him effectively balance work and time with his family, even when things were a little tight. Dad once wrote to me:

"You should recognise that your ability to fuse work and play in everything that you do is something that nobody can take from you, unless you thoughtlessly give it away. The beauty of a holistic attitude towards work and play will turn out to be that the more that you learn how to play at your work, the better the products of your work will naturally be, without having to worry about your work at all."

It is because of this attitude that I have always loved to work. Even when I was young, work was not something to dread; it was yet another arena to learn, to grow and to express myself through my own unique talents. Dad's attitude towards **accountability** is one that I probably appreciate most. As children, we were bound to make mistakes, as all children do; it's a natural part of the process of growing up. The difference is that when we made mistakes, excuses were not tolerated; only a willingness to accept responsibility and come up with solutions to our challenges was suitable.

Mom, on the other hand, is the perfect ying to Dad's yang. Her capacity to find the silver lining in *any* dark cloud is remarkable. She is always smiling, always supportive, and unlike Dad, her physical discipline seems to come and go like the ocean tide. She used to hide candy bars in the freezer on occasion to eat in secret after a healthy meal of tuna fish and cottage cheese salad. She exercised … sometimes. She watched her diet … sometimes, and her optimism towards starting a new lifestyle regime *every* Monday morning is endearing. She was, and still is, just one of those people that you love to be around.

In her imperfection towards health and fitness is found her perfection at accepting everyone as they are. When I went through my chubby phase as a pre teen, she was always right there with a safety pin or needle and thread if my shirt button looked as if it were going to pop. There was never any criticism, just reassurance that all was as it should be and that I was beautiful *just like I was.* She is the kind of mom that acted as if she had just won the lottery whenever I gave her a hand-made card.

In regards to my scholastic achievements, my father always wanted me to do my best. If my grades were not what they should be, he wanted to know if I had given my best effort. If not, I was to work harder next time. When it came to my grades, I tended to be overly optimistic, and I attribute that quality to my mother. I remember coming home once in grade school after a very tough test, having to face my parents with the results. When asked how I had done, I responded cheerfully, "I got the third highest F in the class!"

Mom went into fits of laughter and said that I had just named the title of my first book, as Dad looked on with "the face" – *you all know the one*. Mom's gracious nature and her attitude of gratitude played such a huge role in the person that I have strived to become, and the balance and stability that she and my father created in our household were their greatest gift as parents.

Wrestling with My Faith

When I was eleven, I decided that even though I didn't really "get" the whole Christianity thing, I was sick of being the only one in my group at church that wasn't baptised. In the Baptist faith, it is up to the individual to decide when he or she accepts the Lord as personal saviour. I simply could not get my head around the idea that the only people who got to go to heaven were the ones that believed in Jesus Christ. This was so different than what I knew in my heart to be true. I allowed peer pressure to get the best of me and decided to take the plunge (actually the dip, I suppose). When I came forward to make my proclamation, I was "introduced" to the church (they'd known me all of my life) and asked a few questions. One of these questions happened to be about my hobbies. I immediately responded with WWF Wrestling: the cheesy, wrestling programme on Saturday night TV *and* that I aspired to be the first female quarterback for the Dallas Cowboys. How cute; they all laughed, but the reality was that I didn't have a clue why I was up there. It just didn't make sense to me that they all believed that making this proclamation of faith, followed by the symbolic dunk in the water, was the *only* ticket to heaven.

At eleven, I was trying to save my soul from a place I didn't even believe in, but hey, when in Rome. Despite my apathy, there was one deciding factor that caused me to make the walk that day. A girl in the church who was the same age as me had been taking communion for nearly a year. I couldn't bear it every Sunday when she got to have the wafers and the grape juice like all of the grown ups. It had nothing to do with the body or blood of Christ; this girl got snacks right in the middle of church and yours truly *did not*! I was certain that she had no more of a clue than I did as to why she was receiving communion. This hostility reared its ugly head on the night that little Annie Whelan made her walk of faith. The minister had just finished the sermon and as the last hymn was played, he asked anyone that was ready to take the Lord Jesus Christ as saviour to come forward. Well, up shot Annie Whelan, and I was absolutely mortified! In the last words that I was to speak for a while, I shouted out from the back pew of a packed church, "She's doing it for the juice and the bread!"

I never got spanked much as a child; *never*, according to my brother, Jon, but boy did I get it that night! The preacher's daughter was already building quite the little reputation for herself.

Laying Foundations

In no way do I want to make a mockery of the religion in which my parents brought us up. While a lot of things didn't seem to click with my own personal experiences, the power of group bonding and community did. I learned all about living a life of service and the importance of giving. My love for music has been one of the greatest gifts that going to church gave to me, as I had the opportunity to learn to read music, play instruments and perform in public by Mr. Chapman, one of the most outstanding musicians I have ever met to this day. I was a testament to the fact that learning through osmosis is possible. I spent a lot of time in the hallway listening to the music through the door because I talked incessantly during choir practice and had to be put out on a regular basis. Still, I adored him and was delighted when he eventually married the beautiful piano player that used to giggle at my antics from behind the sheet music. I also learned about the importance of stewardship from a dedicated youth minister named Nancy. I discovered that being a church going teen-ager could still be cool from David, a very hip young minister that brought fresh new ideas about making worship fun.

I came to realise that the church, in and of itself, was not a complete structure, only a foundation on which to build. It was also where I really learned that *all* people are fallible, regardless of faith. The confines of a church can bring out the very best and the very worst in human beings. It is often blamed on the religion itself, but no matter what the religion, people are simply going to make mistakes.

While I no longer subscribe to any particular organised religion, it saddens me to see people throw the baby out with the bath water when they think that their religion has let them down. On the contrary, the mistakes and misjudgements made by the church throughout history have provided more opportunity for personal growth than most realise. It is in the understanding of these shortcomings that we can gain the most spiritual enlightenment.

The awe-inspiring power behind the statement "when two or more are gathered in his name" became obvious. The true potential, the real power of a church congregation, is held in its ability to pray together. The chance to gather as a collective unit, warts and all, sending love, energy and hope into the cosmos, is a miraculous ability that is often misunderstood, even by those who do it.

Chapter 4

The truth of children's wisdom, the health and vitality they experience and the simplicity of their awakening serve as a model to us all, inspiring us and giving us the courage to begin our own Journeys. - **Brandon Bays**

What Dreams May Come

I spent a good part of my childhood experiencing that which is found in most people's memories of growing up: the physical and emotional bumps and bruises, dealing with family and friends, humour and heartache and learning about traditions, faith and religion. At the same time, I seemed to be experiencing a parallel existence. Daytime wasn't all that unusual, but night time, on the other hand, was full of experiences that were unique. I spent night after night outside my body, soaring above the neighbourhood, visiting familiar faces and sometimes not so familiar places. This had become a regular ritual.

Sleep was always such a strange thing for me. Most of the time I avoided sleep for fear of, perhaps, missing something. In actuality, my greatest adventures unfolded while my body slept. While there have been thousands of theories as to what happens when we dream, I don't think science will ever be able to produce a definite answer. Objective science struggles to answer that which is subjective, and while they may be able to pinpoint what happens to the physical body during sleep, no one will ever be able to validate, or discredit, the individual experiences had by our *energetic bodies.*

Exiting my body was as common to me as dreaming "normal" dreams; however, I was well able to distinguish between the two, as each possessed very distinct and individual characteristics. Normal dreaming, which most people are familiar with, created stories that could be based on fact or fantasy. Some say it is the subconscious mind processing the vast amount of information that we are bombarded with every day. Dreams are thought to be some kind of built-in mechanism to sort through and dissipate massive amounts of stimuli. Whatever they are, they are part of who we are, and our feeble attempts to decipher them may never be realised.

Separation from the body while sleeping is a totally different kettle of fish. In my experience, out-of-body travel during sleep never resembled what I came to know as normal dreaming. There were no stories, only real scenarios in which I observed this side of life and spoke to other beings living in extraordinary places which I had yet to experience when awake. The realms that can be reached while out of body are difficult to explain to those who have never practised astral projection. As a child, I did not know the implications of this ability, nor did I know that everyone else *wasn't* doing it, or remembering it, just like me.

The Dog Days of Summer

As well as being a minister and Assistant Principal, my dad was also the head football coach of our local high school team. The mascot for Martinsville High was the mighty Bulldog. School spirit was abundant in those days, and my greatest ambition as a small child was to own my very own Bulldog. When my parents thought that I was old enough for the responsibility, I became the proud mother of Otto Von Bismarck, the beautiful fawn-coloured pedigree of Royal lineage. I loved this dog, and while I left most of the burden of parenting this pet on my poor folks, I adored this animal. He represented my school pride; my first real responsibility in life and all of my dreams come true.

During Otto's first summer with us, I went away to camp for a week with my church youth group. We left on a Sunday, and on the Wednesday that followed, I awakened in the night with a jolt, jumped down from the top bunk and ran out of my cabin. I hadn't a care for disturbing the twenty other campers who were asleep at the time. My camp counsellors woke up and came running into the rain after me. I was headed up the hill, to the main building, insisting on using the phone to call my parents. The girls managed to calm me down long enough to find out what was so upsetting. I proceeded to tell them of my horrible dream, where my precious dog, Otto, had been wheeled into an animal hospital with all four legs up in the air. Men in gowns and masks were frantically working over him, when all of a sudden his legs went limp and he fell over. I sobbed as I told these strangers that my best friend was dead! The counsellors told me that it was just a bad dream. It *was* the middle of the night, and they wouldn't let me call home unless it was an absolute emergency. They said if I was still upset in the morning, they would let me speak to my parents.

First thing the following morning, I rang home only to be told that Otto was fine. Mom and Dad said they loved me, to enjoy the rest of camp, and that they would pick me up on Saturday. Those next three days dragged on as I couldn't wait to get home. Because even at that age, I knew that my dreams were out of the ordinary and that something was seriously wrong. Mom and Dad picked me up that Saturday morning with hugs and smiles and no mention of Otto. Every time I asked about him, they changed the subject.

To this day, I will never forget arriving home, being sat down on the edge of my parent's bed, and told that my sweet little Otto had contracted a "doggy disease" that damaged his brain. It was then they told me that, in fact, he *had* died during the week, but they didn't want to ruin camp by telling me over the phone.

I have never doubted the accuracy of my dreams.

A Shot in the Dark

One Friday afternoon, when I was around eleven or twelve, I had just been to the doctor to receive a booster vaccination. He told my mother the usual.

"She may feel feverish, sore and tired. Just give her some aspirin and she'll be fine."

My father was coaching a football game that night and my mom left me at the home of some family friends while she went to the game. I remember the man carrying me into the house because I felt so unwell. Mom genuinely thought I was just sluggish from the shot, and went on to the game, not realising what was about to take place. This couple did all sorts of things to try to entertain me and "liven" me up. They even made a hat out of a newspaper for me to wear.

I was lying on the couch, paper hat perched on my head, when all of a sudden, I looked down, and I was looking at me. I appeared to be asleep at the time, but I could see all of me, head to toe. This was an unusual sight when you are only accustomed to seeing parts of yourself, or your reflection in the mirror. I remember having a bit of a look around the house, then outside. The experience was similar to leaving my body while asleep, but still, this felt different. This time, I was aware that something wasn't right. And unlike my spirit leaving my body on mid–night adventures, I seemed to be fixated on the fact that I was looking at my own body and that something was seriously wrong with it.

Next thing I knew, my mother was standing next to the couch. I tried to explain what happened, but they all laughed. I felt a bit like Dorothy trying to explain "the land of Oz" to her family after the tornado. They said that I must have been dreaming. Were they kidding? Who did they think they were dealing with, here?

I knew that I had experienced some sort of reaction to the vaccine, and it had temporarily kicked me out of my body. I wasn't afraid because the sensation was so familiar and I finally figured out what was different; it was the first time I had recalled *looking back* at my body after exiting it. I often wonder how many others have experienced these things, but have brushed them off as dreams or flights of fancy.

Chapter 5

Living the new spiritual awareness is a matter of passing through a series of steps or revelations. Each step broadens our perspective. But each step also presents its own set of challenges; it is not enough to merely glimpse each level of expanded awareness. We must intend to live it, to integrate each increased degree of awareness into our daily routine. It only takes one negative interpretation to stop everything. - **James Redfield**

My Public Life goes Private

As far as traumas go, compared to what so many children in the world have faced, I sailed through childhood with no major challenges. My family was solid, we were always provided for, and most of all, we were loved. In my own experience, only a couple of things stand out as significant. One of these was when my father retired from coaching. I loved football, I loved the Martinsville Bulldogs, but most of all, I loved being the coach's daughter. At the time, I valued it as my actual identity. The other momentous emotional upset was when my father decided to leave the public school system in order to become Headmaster of a dwindling private school.

For our family, it was a fantastic move. Dad had the chance to use his remarkable motivational skills to rebuild a struggling school and turn it into a thriving institution. For my ego, it was a nasty blow. I had grown up with the same kids from kindergarten, straight through to the tenth grade. I had forged lasting friendships and experienced life through all of my childhood with the same exact group. Although I was given the choice, I was *strongly* encouraged to finish my last two years of high school with a new bunch of kids in the private school. I was fifteen at the time, a little overweight, and well established with my position amongst my lifelong pals as class clown. I was extremely conscious of what it would mean to redefine my role, attempting to fit in with a new group of peers. To me, private school equated families with lots of money and kids with clothes and cars that my parents couldn't afford. It also meant being in class with everyone who had paid to be there, knowing that the only reason I was there was because my dad was Headmaster.

I wallowed in self-inflicted misery for a while, until reason kicked in and I began to see this as an opportunity. I had the chance to be in smaller classes, play different types of sports than I had in public school, and since there was no cheerleading squad, I could start one *and* be its captain. It's funny how I perceived their world as so shallow, when it was actually me that was lacking substance. While I missed the atmosphere that can only be found in a big high school; the pep rallies, the marching bands, and the huge crowds at all sporting events, I found myself surrounded by new ideas and new ways of learning. While the transition was a little bumpy, I worked my way into this different world and carved a nice little niche for myself.

Oh, Boys!

When I reached my final year in high school, a prerequisite for graduation was to do a "senior project." This was a faculty-approved subject of our choice. It required the seniors to pick a topic, research it, and participate through active involvement. The project began in the spring and finished with each of us presenting our experiences to the entire student body at the end of the school year. Some of my friends chose music or arts. One girl worked at a camp for children with Cancer. Being seventeen and quite an opportunist, I thought my fellow students would greatly benefit from a better understanding of what life was like for young men in military academies (Yes, I'm serious!).

My gruelling research would force me to spend several weeks at *two* different boy's preparatory schools and a week at The United States Naval Academy, where my brother, Jon, was completing his final year. It would be tough, but for the sake of "higher education," I took the task on. I had spent the entire summer and the previous year dieting and running in order to shed my baby fat which had matured in to teen-age fat. I was feeling very good about myself in those days, and lapped up the attention, as the *only* young lady on *all male* campuses could.

The first military academy I visited was less than an hour from home, so I would drive over every day to sit in on classes and interview the cadets about life in the academy. It was during this week that I was introduced to an absolutely gorgeous young man with the most beautiful brown eyes and heart melting smile. Destiny would dictate that he would become the centre of my universe for the summer, nearly two years later, in the small town where I went to college, two States away from where we had first met. Looking back at that relationship, I can see such a classic example of the "sliding doors" theory. How life could have been so different had I pursued my heart, stepped through a different doorway and told him at twenty, that I did, in fact, love him.

Over two decades later, we had the opportunity to reconnect and I experienced the phenomenon that time had changed nothing, only our appearances. As we reminisced about the good old days, we pondered what would have happened if we hadn't moved on and lost touch. Would I have still had the car accident that so profoundly changed my life? Would I have had the experience of dying and returning with the capacity to heal? Would all of this have still happened but in a different way, in different locations under different circumstances if this was, in fact, my chosen life path? Or, could he have become the husband I would divorce years down the line?

The time I spent at that school was important to me on an entirely different level, providing the groundwork for my understanding of the meaning of synchronicity and encountering soul mates, even if only for a brief moment. Not quite what my teachers would be prepared to hear in my presentation to the school!

It happened that my father had been Commandant, Commander and Chief at the second prep school many years earlier, so I had no problem being allowed to move freely about campus doing my "research." Fork Union Military Academy had an outstanding history of academic, athletic and military achievement. The home of the current Commandant also had a past rich with ghost stories. The occupants of this curious, old structure were lifelong friends of my parents. This was to be my home away from home while I *slaved away*, finding out what made the boys of F.U.M.A. tick.

The Commandant's house, Careby Hall, had once been the summer residence of Dr. William E. Hatcher, a Southern Baptist minister known for his great love of socialising and "spirited" spiritual gatherings. He was also a man who witnessed first hand the atrocity that pitted brother against brother, black against white, countrymen against their own: a period in history known as the American Civil War.

The house, built in 1896, had been named for the Hatcher ancestral home in Lincolnshire, England. After retiring from the ministry, Dr. Hatcher took up full-time residence at Careby Hall. He would often look across the oak groves and think that the beautiful slope of land just beyond would make a "splendid place for a school." After raising the five hundred dollars necessary to secure a teacher and premises, Fork Union Academy was born, October 15, 1898. Over one hundred years later, Dr. Hatcher's dream remains a thriving reality, as a Military Preparatory School that has churned out some of America's many outstanding athletes, military leaders and businessmen.

Throughout the years, there have been numerous accounts of something peculiar at Careby Hall. These sightings have been in the form of strange noises, whistling, ghostly apparitions; even dogs standing on their hind legs as if being affectionately patted by an invisible master. Many of these visions were seen in the top window of the tower, situated on the front of the house. Dr. Hatcher's study had previously occupied the space during its hay day of fabulous parties, which drew crowds from all over the South. This house would prove to be of more interest during my stay at Fork Union than my original reason for being there.

I was introduced on my first day to a very handsome cadet, a star player on the football team. I casually turned up at football practice wearing my new, black leather mini skirt and fabulous pink top. Never mind it was nearly 100 degrees and the leather had all but melted to my skin. I thought I looked great *and* I got loads of attention! Thinking back, the attention I was getting was most likely laughter and snide remarks about how stupid I looked in a black leather skirt in the blazing heat!

Anyway, my new acquaintance was given orders to show me around during my stay and to answer any and all questions I had on military life. It was tough work, let me tell you, but we got through it, all the same. Every evening, we would walk around campus and town, and then he would take me back to the Commandant's house, where I would await my goodnight kiss, as he nervously scanned the premises for his Commander and Chief.

One balmy evening, we were tucked behind the bushes "discussing my project" when I happened to look up into the small window on the top floor of the house. I directed my friend's attention up to the window, where as clear as day, I could see the image of a little boy looking down out of the window with a very sad little face. This apparition quickly turned into that of a much larger man. Before

I could let the gasp out of my mouth, I saw a cloud of dust, as my companion had fled the scene – late for curfew, no doubt.

That same week, I was in my room (a beautiful example of Southern finery, with its four poster bed and antique furniture) getting ready for bed. I had gone to the bathroom to brush my teeth. When I came back to the room, the previously closed window was now open. These were no ordinary windows. These were "Gone with the Wind" style – heavy, wooden windows that stuck going up and jammed even worse coming down. I asked my host family if they had opened the window. They just laughed and said it must have been the ghost.

"Great" I said. "That's really what I wanted to hear before bed time!"

I went back to my room, closed the window and climbed into bed. I had been asleep for a while when I noticed I was feeling a little chilly. I sat up, only to see the window open again, and this time all of my blankets were at the foot of the bed. A little spooked, I closed the window *again* and got back into bed, pulling the blankets up around me. I was still awake when I became very aware of a presence in the room. Not only was it in my room, but on my bed, stroking my hair as I lay there very still. I jerked up with a shot, and just as I did, watched all of my blankets being yanked down to the end of the bed.

Funny enough, I wasn't really scared, only startled. I politely, but firmly asked this entity to stop messing with me and to let me get some sleep. I was obliged and nothing else happened after my request for some peace, that night. The next morning, when I told my hosts about the previous evening's ghostly antics, they just laughed as if it was no big deal. It was actually comforting to be in the company of people who had experienced too many paranormal events to dismiss them as anything other than normal. I felt right at home, perfectly at ease, and thoroughly enjoyed my time with that ghost and in that house.

My senior project was amazing, not because I reported any earth-shattering news to my fellow students and faculty, but because I had begun to realise how lucky I was. I had been blessed my whole life with regular contact from the spirit world. No matter where I went, there it was. I always had constant reassurance that I was never alone. I had grown so much in my ability to perceive, but most importantly in my ability to listen, without fear. I was truly beginning to understand that no experience in my life was without reason, or purpose.

I was also learning that once we are given a new concept or knowledge, the opportunity to use it lays waiting, just around the corner.

Chapter 6

Life is a journey of either Fate or Destiny. Fate is the result of giving in to one's wounds and heartaches. Your destiny unfolds when you rise above the challenges of your life and use them as Divine opportunities to move forward, to unlock your higher potential. **- Caroline Myss**

Falling From the Nest

I was in the process of deciding the future of my next level of education. I really wanted to follow in my sister's footsteps, attending James Madison University. JMU was in Harrisonburg, Virginia, and my sister, Beth, had studied graphic design there ten years earlier. I also wanted to study graphic design, and I think familiarity with the school was dictating my decision, not to mention its great reputation for being a massive party school.

One day I was hanging out in the Senior Lounge during my final months as a high school student, when I was called to my father's office. Earlier that day, Dad had heard a familiar voice outside of his office door, and when he looked out, he was greeted by an old friend that he had coached football with many years earlier. This man was now the President of a small, private college in South Carolina, and was on a visit to recruit new students to his school. When I went into Dad's office, I was introduced to his friend as a prospective candidate.

I was a little shocked; I had more or less made up my mind to go to James Madison, and my dad knew it. I suppose he wanted me to consider the possibility, as this was a prestigious school, and the President was offering me a partial academic scholarship as incentive to attend. There was a weekend coming up to show students around the college, so my father and I decided that I would attend. I figured I would have a look, just to please my folks, but in my mind, I was JMU bound.

In exchange for entertaining the possibility of attending this college, the one stipulation was that my parents let me attend this weekend *on my own*. I wanted to have a proper look, without their influence, and as an eighteen year-old that had never strayed from my parent's protection I was determined to give the college scene a good go. I arrived at Coker College on a Friday afternoon to attend the welcome dinner party that evening. Much to my surprise, I was the *only* prospective student who had not been accompanied by their parents. We met some of the Coker students that night and the usual college rituals of drinking and partying commenced. I had never been around anything like it. The next day was full of activities trying to entice us to choose this small, but very lively school, but all of us were eagerly waiting for the night time shenanigans to begin.

Each visiting student had been paired up with a buddy for the weekend. My buddy was responsible for "looking after me," sharing her room, as well as introducing me to the college experience. Just imagine the excitement I felt, first time away from the nest, with guys and girls living in the same dorms and alcohol everywhere I turned!

I was not an experienced drinker at all. I came from a household where alcohol never crossed our threshold, not even on special occasions. I had never really indulged, so even a little bit was way too much to drink for me. That night, I found myself in a situation that would change the direction of my entire life.

There were students gathered all through the hallways, drinking and smoking, with music blaring. A guy that had been flirting with me all night, took me by the hand, led me down the hall and said he wanted to show me something. No *really*, that's what he said and yes, I *really* did go. Sheer stupidity was now dictating my every move.

I was well intoxicated at this stage; letting this guy lead me into a darkened room, where suddenly, I became aware that we were not alone. I could just make out the face of another person from the light of the bathroom next door. Before I knew what was happening, I was being stripped by two pairs of hands and pushed to the floor. I screamed for help but no one could hear me over the loud music and laughter. The next few minutes were a terrifying blur, as I realised that every parent's worst nightmare was happening to me, and there was absolutely *nothing* I could do to stop it.

Somehow, sometime later, I made it back to my buddy's room, and passed out. I awoke the next morning with a very sick head and the horrific realisation of what had happened the night before. I never mentioned to anyone what went on that night, and I did not see my assailants before I left. Being Sunday, it was the final day of my weekend visit, so after a few very brief goodbyes, I got in my car and made the four hour trip home.

The journey down had been much different. I was full of anticipation, singing at the top of my lungs to Aerosmith on the radio. Going home, I drove in complete silence. In the space of those four hours, I made the foremost decisions that were to completely alter the course I had previously chosen for my life. I accepted the fact that I was partially responsible for what had happened to me, because *I had made the decision to drink that night* and was unable to take care of myself. Accountability had been drummed into me my entire life, so when I arrived home, I marched into the house, a big smile on my face and announced to my parents,

"I'm starting at Coker College in the fall!

I never told my parents what happened that weekend, not because I was embarrassed or ashamed, but because on the drive home, I had created an agenda that became a very personal, calculated mission. I know that Mom and Dad would have been devastated, and so hurt for me, yet fully supportive. However, I was not going to let the obvious concerns that any parent would have had in this situation prevent me from carrying out *my plan*. As far as I was concerned, I had gone from teenager to woman overnight. It was my responsibility to clean up my own mess. At the time it all happened, I suppose I was disappointed in myself for straying so far from the thoughtful and loving boundaries in which I had been raised and for being so naive that I allowed my safety to be compromised.

I didn't permit myself to wallow in these feelings for long though, because I had also been taught that living in remorse and regret stood to destroy me quicker than any lapse in good judgement ever could.

Looking back at this decision, I know I did what I thought was best for me at the time. As a parent, I hope that if anything like this ever happened to one of my daughters, they would choose to tell me. If they didn't, I would understand, and I really mean that. I can honestly say I wouldn't have done it differently. I was learning and experiencing life within the confines of the knowledge and 'street smarts' that I had acquired during my eighteen years on Earth, limited as they were. This was a key time in my growth and development as a human being, and to wish that time to be any different *now,* would mean that part of me was still there, being raped spiritually and emotionally, over and over again.

That brief point in time of physical pain and humiliation pales in comparison to a lifetime of bitterness and regret.

This experience, and *every* other experience I have had, has helped to shape the person that I am today. To identify myself at any point in my life as a rape victim was, and is, unthinkable. I choose to identify myself as the ongoing production of *all* of my life's experiences. To single out any one experience, be it "good," or "bad," and wear it as a badge of identity, immediately takes a person out of the present and places a portion of their essence, *their very life force*, in the past. Good choices, bad choices: In the end, they are our own personal decisions and there are no wrong decisions. When you believe that ultimately there are no accidents, every situation in life has *potential*.

It is difficult to regret the outcomes of the choices we have made, if we own them rather than allowing them to own us. Potential, I think, is a very misunderstood phenomenon. We seem to think that if a situation doesn't work out the way we want it to, then its potential has been wasted or expressed negatively. I feel that potential means that *any* situation has the ability to change life dramatically. It is up to the individual and her or his interpretation of an event to determine what way life will be affected by the choices that are made.

Therefore, potential is neither positive nor negative, good or bad; it simply is what we make of it.

Chapter 7

There is no discouragement like the discouragement that comes from self generated wrongdoing. Enduring the consequences of one's own irresponsibility creates feelings of grief and guilt that defy description. It is a very bitter experience to know that suffering need not have been; that it has resulted from indiscretion and inconsistency; that it is the harvest of one's own sewing; that the vulture which feeds on the vitals is a vulture that you have created. **That is real pain**. The laws of the heart, the home, of the soul and of human life, cannot be violated without great pain, to someone. **- Dick Hensley**

The Wrong Way to be Right

In August of 1987, I began studies at the small, private college in Hartsville, South Carolina. My parents went with me to help move me in to my new home on a very hot, late-summer evening. When I was all settled into my dorm room, I bid my parents farewell and began a new chapter in my life as a college student. They were going home, for the first time in thirty-five years with no birds in the nest. I'm sure it is an unusual time for parents, with feelings of elation and pride, laced with panic and fear, as they watch their children strike out on their own for the very first time. While I should have been full of anticipation, meeting new friends, looking forward to a fresh approach to education, I was instead focused on a very personal agenda.

The Sunday night before classes began there was a big party in my dorm. A guy in my class, who had been a gymnast in high school, was showing off, walking up and down the hallway on his hands. A bunch of us were cheering him on, when we all heard a loud *crack*! I looked around to see what had happened when I saw everyone rushing towards me. I put my hand up to my face and felt my nose bleeding like a tap and looked down and my fabulous new outfit that was quickly being destroyed with blood. Only then did I hit the floor!

Our gymnast friend had kicked his legs up to begin walking on his hands again, when he made a direct hit to my nose!

The hospital was across the road from the college, and I ended up spending the rest of the night there. I was the proud new owner of a broken nose, set in a ridiculous looking plaster, topped off with two, swollen, black eyes. A marvellous look for my first day of college!

I made it through the day, feeling remarkably well, despite my scary appearance. I was not going to miss this day, not because it was my first day of college, but because there were two young men who needed to know *I was back.* I saw both of them that day, veterans of the college scene, chatting to all of the new girls, staking their claims as "Big Men on Campus." Imagine their shock as they first realised that the freshman girl with the mangled face *wasn't exactly a stranger.* The worst mistake these boys had ever made had just come back to haunt them. Phase One was complete.

I would see both of these boys on a daily basis. Sometimes in class, at every meal, and they always seemed to disappear when we attended the same parties. I never spoke to them, only gave them each a knowing nod, and a smile from time to time. I was systematically wearing them down, and the agony of never knowing what my next move would be finally became too much for one of them to bear. He came to me towards the end of my first year, riddled with guilt and having become seriously ill over the last few months from the stress of it all. He broke down in tears and apologized for an act that he could never justify. The second fellow just seemed to disappear from the campus. Phase Two and Three were now, finally over.

I'm sure many would feel that I should have turned them in to the school and the police. In my heart, I knew that although what they had done was horribly cruel, my actions and the way I handled the circumstances could change the course of both of their lives, just as theirs had changed mine. Some may say that they got away with it. I felt they got away with nothing. Watching the person you have wronged get on with life can sometimes be a harsher punishment than any they could have received from the school or the law. But behind the façade of my nobility, *I had made a gross error.*

In the beginning, my objectives were not as dignified as they were by the time that both boys were out of my daily life. Luckily, I realised that I obviously had not let go of the experience completely, because I was attached to *how they responded* by seeing me "get on with life." I thought I was so advanced because of the way I was dealing the situation, when in actuality, having any interest at all in how they perceived me meant that they still *had* me, and that I still had something to prove.

Eventually, they both could no longer live with the day-to-day reality of their grave, drunken error and both, in the end, chose to change their own life directions. I had been in control of my decision to attend the college, *but for what reason?* Their lives seemed to spiral out of control the minute I returned. That had been my objective. My life *had* moved on, and I thought I *was* a better person for it, but *only* until I had discovered that it was *my* thought process that needed to change.

This had started out as an exercise in revenge, but thank heavens, it didn't finish that way. If it had, I would surely have been the loser. I was so fortunate that in the end I had realised that this opportunity had been created as a chance for me to show myself, and no one else, the stuff I was made of.

Unconditional love coupled with releasing the past is a lesson that can only be learned when an individual is faced with the greatest adversity.

These abilities are not learned from a book or a class, only from life experience itself. I am always hesitant to use the word "forgiveness," replacing it with "releasing the past," in that it implies that someone has harmed you, and therefore is in need of your forgiveness. *We can never be harmed by another if we **truly** grasp the enormity of this concept.* This is not to say that we should knowingly place ourselves in dangerous situations, and that intervention should not be used when necessary. In my own situation, I knew in my heart that no one had hurt me. Neither my psyche, nor my soul had been damaged. I also knew that in this case, two young men had got themselves caught up in a terrible situation: too much booze, coupled with a very gullible and vulnerable target. I'm sure that my life would have progressed differently had I chosen to remain in the role of victim. I was carelessly headed that way, fooling myself that the silent torture that I was subjecting these boys to was hurting them, not me.

Deep in my heart, I realised that this would not serve me, and I also eventually discovered that the unconditional love and forgiveness was something I needed to give to myself, *no one else*. Their actions were not mine to punish, even though I chose to see how the Universe, rather than the law, would deal with their conduct. *The big joke is that I thought this was about them.*

I share this excerpt of my past, not for sympathy, a pat on the back or for criticism of my choices. I merely want to show that sometimes what is perceived as a horror in the past is just that – *in the past*. I am able to speak and write about this experience as a fact, something that took place along my journey. It has no positive or negative charge for me — no anger, no shame, no pride and no regret. I do not tell this story to show you my wounds; there are no wounds to show, *only experience*. And this was an experience that holds no more clout than any other I share in this book. All of them are part of me yet no single one defines me. The power of living in the moment is unparalleled. Making the move from "an eye for an eye" type of justice to compassion for human error, *including your own*, is liberating.

To live in the past is a treacherous curse that stifles the human experience. Even more debilitating is the lack of courage to admit when we are wrong. Not wrong because something was done to us, but wrong to hang on to it, allowing it to make us bitter and disempowered.

Chapter 8

Far better it is to dare mighty things, to win glorious triumphs, even though checkered by failure, than to take rank with those poor spirits who neither enjoy much nor suffer much because they live in the grey twilight that knows neither victory nor defeat. - **Theodore Roosevelt**

Head over Heels

That first year of college was to offer many new adventures, some fantastic and others fantastically painful. I was quickly coming to the realisation that the happily ever after of fairy tales was not quite what it was cracked up to be. The idea of the beautiful princess awaiting her one true love, unscathed by life and adored by all, was replaced with self-consciousness, a poor body image and a struggle to conform to people and activities that really held no interest for me. Suddenly, the outstanding qualities that had made me such a unique and interesting child were now a liability. I couldn't see my own inner beauty and did anything and everything just to fit in. I even played soccer that year. I *hated* soccer.

I was never much of an athlete. I was always the one on any sports team who had the outstanding team spirit. I won little awards for being the *sparkplug* or *best team supporter*. A nice gesture, but what they really meant was "we love your attitude, but you really suck!" I never minded being the moral support or *team psychologist*, because I am one of those people who don't really like to get dirty or sweat too much! I had always been a cheerleader in high school and went on to cheer in college for our basketball team. Don't get too excited... it wasn't like the bubble gum movies of American high school cheerleaders, doing back flips from the top of a human pyramid; it was simple, old-fashioned jumping up and down, cheering the team on. The outfits were cute, it required minimal sweating, and my hair always remained perfectly intact. It was the eighties; I had the perm to prove it! Do you know how difficult it is to maintain that kind of hair volume when running up and down a soccer pitch in the sweltering South Carolina heat?

I much preferred to cheer on the sidelines, scanning the crowd and the opposing team for anyone *interesting*. The sidelines were where I should have stayed. As misfortune would have it, several of our soccer players were injured one fateful day, and yours truly was called up by the coach, from the *very end* of the bench, in an act of pure desperation. I stood out like a sore thumb in my pristine uniform, and at this stage in the game, I was most certainly the best looking thing on the field by default. I found myself surrounded by actual athletes: dirty, sweaty, and ready to finish the game they had all started. They weren't going to let me off that field alive! Sure enough, the ball was kicked to me. Just as I went to kick it to someone *who knew* what they were doing, the scariest girl I have ever seen was flying straight for me, teeth gnashed and looking for blood.

The next thing I remember was looking at my foot next to my right ear, wondering "is this possible?" I had moved straight through the peak of pain and into shock – probably because my first and last five minutes of sports fame had left me flat on my back, wounded and dirty, with really bad hair! The cartilage was removed from my knee a few days later, and I was in plaster for the next six weeks. A painful attempt to make new friends, but I did enjoy having my books carried for the next month! Eventually, I took up rowing. I didn't have to use my knees, I got to sit (which didn't make it seem like exercise), my hair always remained reasonably unharmed, and I loved being on the water. Other than that, I never attempted organised sports again.

About the same time as my sports *faux pax*, I was to experience yet another first in my life. I fell in love. It couldn't be as simple as boy meets girl, nope, no fear of that. I had to fall in love with the guy from the next town over who had started his studies at a near by college with dreams of parties, girls and sports, but got his girlfriend pregnant in what was probably the first sexual experience for both of them. He did what he was advised to do, marrying the mother of his child. He had left college to get a job to support his new family and found himself all grown up, before he could even legally vote or take a drink.

Needless to say, these circumstances didn't lend themselves to a fairy-tale romance. Why, one may ask, would I have allowed myself to get involved with this guy? Well, when I met him at a party one night, he didn't exactly introduce himself with "Hi, I'm Josh. I had to drop out of school to marry a girl I got pregnant a few years ago, but I would really like to get to know you "cause I think you're just swell."

It was more like a starry-eyed gaze from across the room, a smile, and then two worlds collided. I was done; hook, line and sinker. He began to court me, picking me up late at night when he finished work and taking me for moonlit strolls in the school's beautiful gardens. It never crossed my mind that my handsome new beau was married, much less, a father. It was weeks before he worked up the courage to confirm the stories that I had begun to hear. When he finally told me that he was, in fact, married I cried for days, because I knew that he could never be truly mine. It took me a while to come to terms with the end of the relationship because I was crazy about him, and at that point in my life, my heart, not my head, ruled my morality. But morality did win in the end, as my self-esteem would not allow me to tread where I did not belong.

Many years later, I made the connection that it was this first year of college that really planted the seeds for the men I seemed to be drawn to and the lessons that I was to attract into my life. I had my first taste of what it felt like for someone to really like me, really want to be with me, but not enough for me to be first in their life. This was the beginning of a pattern that unfortunately forged itself as the blueprint for several of my future relationships.

The Ghost Who Went to School

Coker College began as an all women's school over 100 years ago. It remained that way until it began accepting male day students after World War II. As with many old southern schools, Coker had a resident ghost. All new students were introduced to her legend upon arrival. Many seasoned co-eds had their own stories of encounters with Madeline and loved to shock and amaze the freshmen with the harrowing tales of her tragic death.

Madeline was reported to have been a student in the early years of the twentieth century. She had fallen in love with one of her professors, becoming pregnant during their affair. He was reputed to have shunned her, leaving her on her own to deal with his unborn child. In her distraught state, Madeline hung herself in one of the old dormitories. She has been a significant part of Coker campus lore ever since. Girls have attested to being comforted by a presence in the midst of boyfriend strife, and guys have claimed to be threatened or bothered by this spectre when not treating their women well. She made for great late night gossip and was the catalyst for many practical jokes and midnight séances.

Throughout college, I had a close group of friends that were inseparable. We went to classes together (sometimes), we played sports together (I mostly watched) and we got up to all sorts of mischief together. We had heard tales of a Ouija board, which was supposed to be hidden away in the attic of the dorm where our ghost Madeline had ended her life. The legend goes that a group of students, many years earlier, had attempted to contact Madeline using this game. They apparently got more than they bargained for when her spirit spoke to them, so they hid the board in the attic, never to be played again. Well, of course, curiosity got the best of us. Three of my friends and I went on a reconnaissance mission to find the haunted board game. We *actually* found the old Ouija board tucked away in the attic, and brought it down to my room.

70

I was living in the older dorm, which had not changed much over the years. Big, noisy, old radiators, hardwood floors, a cast iron bathtub with feet, and quite a spacious living area were standard in these rooms. That evening, about ten of us gathered around the coffee table, and my friend Len and I were nominated to do the honours. For those who don't know, a Ouija board is a game board consisting of the alphabet and the numbers one through ten. There is the word yes and the word no.

The players use a pointer – a plastic triangular shape that is meant to move across the board, spelling out names, places, etc. Each person has their fingers lightly placed on the pointer, and questions are then asked to the "spirit world." The pointer then is supposed to glide over the surface to spell out answers and give guidance. It was amusing to push the pointer where you wanted it to go then shout, "Did you see that??? It wasn't me, I swear!!!"

On this particular evening, they couldn't have chosen two greater jokesters in Len and me. Everyone was in for a good night's entertainment with us on the board. We summoned up all of our powers and called upon the spirit of Madeline. The pointer flew around the board a few times (with no help, of course......) and Len proceeded to ask Madeline where she was. The pointer slowly moved to the letter N. Then it moved to M, then H. Back again, to N, to M, then H. Back to N, then to M and H. We were laughing away as I suddenly realised, hang on a second, that is saying "N...MH N...MH...In MH!"

"I'm MH – Mary Helen. Oh crap! Len, would you cut it out!" Then the famous line, "That's not me, I swear!!!" Everyone was in hysterics as my face went from calm and collected to totally freaked out! The one rule of the Ouija board is that no matter what, you are always to sign off. *Never* are you to pull your hands away, even if you get spooked. I can't say that I had the rules in mind; I had had enough and yanked my hands off the board. At that very moment, the full length mirror on the back of my bedroom door shattered into a million

71

pieces. Imagine the screams from ten terrified college kids as we simultaneously realised that no one was even remotely close to that door. That game was packed up fast and thrown back into the attic. The group of us swore never to touch it again, no matter what.

That night we all slept in the same room with the lights on. What actually happened? I've never really been sure, but as true as I am sitting here, it did happen. Ten other people witnessed this event and hold the same memory of our night with the Ouija board.

Innocent fun is what that year was all about. Most of my friends in our circle of ten were originally from somewhere around Atlanta, Georgia, including my roommate, Jani. As the end of the school year approached we couldn't bear the thoughts of living away from our buddies, so we decided that we would venture out into the big, bad world and work for the summer in "Hotlanta". To this day, I still can't believe my parents let me go!

Scattered, Smothered, Covered and Chunked

Jani and I had a very inflated perception of our worth in the working world, assuming that getting high-class, high-paying jobs would be a piece of cake. Our rude awakening came as days turned into weeks of job hunting, and our lofty ideas of moving into our own apartment were getting further and further out of reach. We were sharing a bedroom in Jani's parents apartment with her younger sister; it was cramped, and certainly not the glamorous lifestyle we were seeking. We decided that if we were to achieve our summertime dream of living on our own as "responsible" adults, we had better take the next job available.

The Waffle House is a Southern icon; a haven for travellers and truck drivers in search of a big, juicy burger and hash browned potatoes. Never in my wildest dreams did I envision myself in an orange and brown polyester uniform shouting out orders in a bizarre, cryptic code. "Order up! Hash browns–scattered, smothered, covered and chunked!"

We went to a restaurant not too far from where we were living and took the plunge. We weren't the typical WH applicants. We were nineteen, blonde and very tan college girls. We were hired on the spot to start work the next day on the morning shift, from 7 a.m. to 2 p.m. This suited us perfectly, as it allowed us the entire afternoon off for working on the tans.

The Waffle House, or "Le Chateau de Waffle," as I referred to it when telling my parents about the new restaurant I was working in, was a unique dynasty in its own right. Each unit was ranked on its performance and assigned a number to create competition amongst the individual locations. Jani and I landed in a restaurant that was fairly low on the totem pole, as it was located slightly off the beaten path. However, a funny thing happened that summer in the Waffle House Kingdom.

Some of the main clientele of the world famous Waffle House are truck drivers. These people are an amazing breed, all their own. They spend most of their time on the road communicating over the air waves in a language so off the wall that no one but a fellow trucker could understand. But most of all, they look out for one another. It wasn't too long before word got out about two young blondes, working in a slightly out of the way truckers' delight, and in a matter of weeks our totem pole turned upside down and bottom headed straight for the top. In less than three months, Jani and I made nearly ten thousand dollars in tips and lived in our very own apartment, just outside the big city. When the summer came to an end, the two of us headed to Myrtle Beach, South Carolina, for what we felt was a well deserved break.

In just one week, we spent nearly half of everything we had earned in tips, had some of it stolen, and returned to school with nothing to show but a few fantastic stories.

Forbidden Fruit

Over the summer holidays, friends of mine that had been home to Virginia didn't come back empty-handed like Jani and me. They had brought back a huge batch of homemade moonshine. This brew became the feature of our "Welcome Back to School" party. This was no ordinary moonshine; it had pieces of fruit floating around inside the jar that had been marinating in pure grain alcohol for years. Being totally green about the alcoholic properties of distilled alcohol, curiosity got the best of me. I was too afraid to *drink* the concoction, so I thought I would be *much more sensible* and try a bit of fruit.

I had no idea that an innocent little peach was lethal after years of soaking in alcohol. I would have been better off just drinking the liquor! My friend cut off a sliver of a peach, and I ate it with no apparent side effects. I decided to chance another slice, then another, until I had nearly half a peach down my neck. If I had only waited a few minutes before taking the other slices, I would have realised the potency this peach packed. Instead, I sat down, leaned against a wardrobe, then my head began to spin. I could hear everyone talking, but it wasn't long before I was looking down at myself, slumped over and lifeless. Everyone was laughing and chatting, carrying on around me, under the assumption that I must have passed out.

I distinctly remember hovering in the far top corner of the room looking at my body with complete indifference. I didn't feel scared, worried, or upset. In fact, I knew the body was mine, but did not identify it as the real *me*. I had been out of my body so many times before that it didn't seem abnormal. I was aware, however, that like the time that I had reacted to a vaccination, something was wrong with the body. I hadn't simply projected my spirit outside of the body, I had poisoned it out. As easily as I had exited, I re-entered a short while later. There was no point telling anyone what had happened, because no one would have believed me, and subsequently, I spent the remaining years of college suffering the nickname "Peaches".

Chapter 9

It's my belief that our individual dreams actually connect us far more than many of us imagine. Dreams offer us fleeting glimpses of our human interconnectedness and a shared imagery that we're only now beginning to understand. - **Lisa Lenard**

An Officer and a Gentleman

My sophomore year of college proved to be a very interesting one in terms of my psychic development. That year, I began to have numerous dreams that would eventuate into reality. At first, they were simple enough. I would dream the scores to the basketball games, and they would be accurate. It became a bit of a pastime for my roommate and me. I would dream the scores; we would write them down and seal them in an envelope; go cheer at the game; then come back and have a look. Wouldn't that have come in handy if I was a gambling kind of girl? Even at that early stage in my growing awareness, I instinctively knew that gifts like these were never to be used for personal gain.

As they progressed, my dreams didn't limit themselves to basketball. There was a girl that lived on the floor above me named Kelly. She had lost her father when she was a teen. A sudden illness had taken his life, leaving her quite guarded and serious at a very early age. One day, Kelly came down to ask my roommate and me if we could help her find something she had lost – an earring belonging to a very special pair given to her by her late father. We went to her room and turned the place upside down, but couldn't find the missing piece of jewellery. Needless to say, she was very upset to have mislaid something of such sentimental value, because it could never be replaced.

75

That night as I slept, I was visited in a dream by a man in a uniform. He identified himself as Kelly's father. He told me that he was aware that he would be able to communicate with me, and that he knew that his daughter was very distressed about losing the gift he had given her so many years ago. This life-like apparition told me that the earring had fallen between the floorboards underneath the big radiator in her room. He thanked me for my help, and the dream promptly ended.

The next morning I went straight up to Kelly's room and told her about my dream. She was sceptical, but at this point she was so desperate to find the earring, she went and had a look anyway. Sure enough, there sat her prized possession, exactly where I had told it would be. The interesting thing was, when I explained to Kelly how this man was dressed, she replied, "Well, of course he was. My father was an officer in the military".

Sleepless in South Carolina

It became quite a regular occurrence for me to dream that someone was in trouble or had died. My mother would always be amazed, yet never really surprised, when she would ring to tell me about someone's passing. I would invariably tell her who it was before she could get a word in. As cool as it sounds, knowing these things can be very unnerving. I began to worry that I was going to dream the demise of one of my family members or close friends. Since the only time that this was happening was when I was asleep, it seemed logical at the time that if I refrained from sleeping, I wouldn't get this information. So, for the remainder of my second year of school, I became a self-inflicted insomniac, catching cat naps during the day, and sleeping little to none during the night.

One can only imagine the effect this had on my schoolwork. I was majoring in graphic design as well as communications. I spent many late nights in the art department, and the rest of my studies went down the tubes. My ideas for art were good enough, but the ability to implement them when running on fumes began to show. I did very poorly in school that year and did everything I could to hide this fact from my parents.

I had turned into quite the prankster. I suppose I had too much free time on my hands at night while everyone else was sleeping. My partner in crime and fellow Ouija board connoisseur, Len, was always around to help carry out my cunning plots. He never seemed to sleep a lot either, so we had loads of fun devising new schemes to create chaos and excitement around campus. Somehow, no matter what mischief happened at that school, Len and I always got the blame.

Trials and Tribulation

Coker College had decided to implement a points system to punish the college students. Crimes ranged from drinking underage to parking illegally on campus. The punishments or points, as they were called, didn't seem to match the offences. A total of thirty points resulted in disciplinary proceedings, which could result in expulsion from school. For instance, a couple of parking tickets and a beer at twenty, as opposed to twenty-one, could put a student's education in an early grave. The college hired a woman to live in the dorms to police the student's activities.

Now this gal was perfect for the job, because she had obviously forgotten how just a few short years ago, she, too, had been a college student. For some strange reason she never really "took" to me. One of her jobs was to always remain in the dorms after midnight, in case of student emergencies. Someone had heard that she had been sneaking out at night to visit a "friend". Someone also thought it would be great to catch her in the act and make her sweat a little when she crept back

77

to her room in the wee hours. As legend has it, a little bit of super glue found its way into the lock of her bedroom door, and her quiet re-entry became an early morning fiasco. As usual, Len and I were the first suspects. I got a lot of penalty points for this little episode, even though there were no fingerprints or DNA recovered! On top of a few parking tickets, and a random beer sighting, I was dangerously close to the disciplinary limit, but somehow managed to keep it together until Spring Break.

Spring in South Carolina was just when the temperatures started to rise, and it was stinking hot in those old dorms. I was to turn in my final art project at eight a.m., which meant staying up most of the night to get it done. Len's room had air-conditioning, and I had spent most of the day working on my project in his room. I moved back to my room that night because one of the points system offences was cohabitation, defined as guys and girls in the same room after midnight. Now, this went on all night *every* night in most rooms, but I wasn't about to push my luck that close to the end of the year, when my slate would be wiped clean for my junior year.

I went back to my quarters when I realised that I had left my glue stick up in Len's room and would be unable to complete the assignment without it. I ventured back to the room, knocked on the door and asked Len to give me my glue. Just then, I heard, "We've got you now!"

And there she stood, the dorm mistress of the dark, with a few of her cronies, and for the first time, I remember seeing her smile. I was cheerfully awarded my points and was left to be dealt with on return from Spring Break.

I was called into the President's office when school reopened and told that my parents were being called and that I was to be dismissed from school! As the system allowed, I was given a trial by the student council, which took place a few days later. The President agreed not to call my folks until after the trial, just in case, by a long shot, it went in my favour.

The next few days at school can only be described as one of those teenage, Hollywood, feel-good films. The number of students that rallied to the cause was staggering. It was Alumni Day on campus at the end of the week, and by the time the old southern darlings of yesteryear arrived, they were greeted by posters, banners and t-shirts put together by my buddies in the art department. A little man in a jail uniform with the Coker logo proudly displayed was the theme of all of these articles of protest. The thing that upset the students the most was the fact that the final nail in my coffin was cohabitation. This was because the phone call my parents would receive, giving the final reason for my expulsion as cohabitation, meant the offence sounded as if I had been caught sleeping around, as opposed to being caught red handed with a glue stick. But as it stood, I was going down for a crime I did not commit.

"Save Mary Helen" was posted all over campus in true *Ferris Beuller's Day Off* fashion! Len was called as a witness to the makeshift trial and sweated it out, as some of our escapades would have jeopardised his soccer scholarship. I stuck it out through the inquisition and to this day stand proud that even though I was offered the chance to remain in school if I "ratted out" some of my friends, I never did. I know that this put my parents through unnecessary hardship, but I was learning lessons of loyalty that have lasted a lifetime. I remain in touch with those people to this day.

The trial came and went, and word spread quickly that I had lost my appeal. I went to the President's office, pleaded my case one last time and watched anxiously as he picked up the phone to call my father. I don't know who was more nervous, me or him, because this was going to be a tough call for the President to make for two reasons – he was a friend of my father, and harder still, my parents didn't have a clue that I was in the slightest bit of trouble. Needless to say, the news went down like a lead balloon. I would have hated to be on the other end of the line as my Dad expressed his deepest disappointment that he and my mother hadn't been informed that their daughter was in so much trouble that her college education was now in jeopardy. My father dealt with the situation before dealing with me, and as the story goes, he *reasoned* me back into school.

My Dad is an absolute master at making somebody, anybody, see his point. As I have matured, I can say without hesitation that most of the time he *was* right. Whatever he said that day got me back in school, *with a few conditions*. I was to move off campus and would not be allowed to do anything but attend classes. No socialising, no athletic events, only education. It was a good thing that I had just had the Spring Break of a lifetime, because it was the last fun I was to have for a while, or so I thought....

Making Waves

The week of Spring Break was spent in the Florida Keys with my roommate, Jani. We had driven down, spending our time between Ft. Lauderdale and Key Largo. Lots of things happened on that wild week away; however, one thing in particular stands out. We met some guys who owned a fishing boat, and they invited us to a party where several boats were tied up to one another but anchored quite some distance from shore. We spent the night hopping from one boat to the next until the party was forced to end. A sudden, violent storm that seemed to come out of nowhere caused the boys to throw us into a speed boat, heading for land. Massive waves knocked us about, tossing the tiny boat around and threatening to take us under. We were in serious danger, but finally managed to make it back. We were all terrified and a bit banged up, but essentially unharmed.

The odd thing about this whole experience was the following day, when I phoned home to check in with my parents. My mother jumped straight on the phone, asking if I was okay. She sounded very relieved to hear my voice. The night before, she had experienced an awful feeling that I was in terrible danger. I assured her that I was fine, and never told her until many years later just how right she had been. This particular incident was interesting, because it's the first time I remember my mother ever having her own encounter with psychic awareness. I suspect she may have very well had other occurrences unbeknownst to me, but this was the first one I had ever witnessed.

There's No Place Like Home

The trouble I had got myself in at school meant I had to return to Virginia for the summer, live at home, work, and take courses at the community college. I now had to make up for how poorly I had done the previous school year. I was dreading going home, mostly from embarrassment. Relations were a touch strained between Dad and myself. When I first landed home, he was disappointed, and rightly so, at the situation I had gotten myself into at Coker. He knew I could do better. I had let no-one down but myself and was feeling a little worse for the wear due to the trouble I was in, as well as from the effects of living with the waking nightmare of insomnia for the last year. *I was feeling a little too sorry for myself to see the lesson that was right in front of my eyes.* After arriving home from work one evening, I found a note from Dad on my bed. It read:

"If you let continuous regret, remorse, self-persecution keep you from functioning now; if you persist indefinitely in feeling guilty and upset over something that is over, then you are behaving in a

non-productive manner. Feeling guilty is not going to make your life any better. You can learn from your mistakes, vow to avoid repeating them, and get on with living NOW."

Eckhart Tolle hadn't even begun writing about *the now* when Dick Hensley popped out with this one! That note meant so much to me that I still have it tucked away in my diary, all these years later.

I made a major attitude adjustment that day and proceeded to have an amazing summer. I reconnected with Beth, one of my closest childhood friends; I had a lot of fun at work; and I managed to excel at community college. I was so excited about my exemplary behaviour that Beth and I decided to host the party of the summer in my parent's house. Mom and Dad had gone away for a weekend and didn't find out about that party until 2003, fourteen years later.

My mother was at home following a knee replacement, the same one she had injured when I was a toddler. The physical therapist who visited her at home casually said one day, "Oh, I haven't been to this house since your daughter had a party here, back in the late eighties —and that was *some* party! I even remember the police coming around because there were so many people there!"

What he, or anybody else at that party *didn't* know, was that I had a friend working in the police department that summer and I had called him myself, to get the floods of partiers out of my parent's house. Even all that time later, the folks *were not* impressed.

Chapter 10

The gift of this planet is that you're surrounded by love, because the definition of love is both sides of experience: praise and reprimand, support and challenge, being lifted up and put down simultaneously. That is divine will. Theology describes it as the right and left hands of the Creator coming down to make sure you're always in balance. When you see and honour this balance, your life is transformed: you're liberated.

- **Dr. John F. Demartini**

A Home of My Own

I returned to Coker in the autumn with a new attitude *and* my own apartment. I had dreaded the thought of living off campus, on my own, away from all of my friends. It turned out to be a life-changing experience, introducing me to a whole new level of freedom. I met an entirely different group of friends, locals from the town of Hartsville. I met a family that took me in as one of their own, and had many strange and wonderful adventures with Mr. and Mrs. Dolan, and their clan. Mr. Dolan was a lawyer and a good old southern gentleman. Mrs. Dolan was an absolute gem. She always loved me because I was a fellow Coker-nut, she having gone to school there when it was still an all-girls school back in the 1940s. I was also forty years younger than her to the day. Even more bizarre, she was from South Carolina and my mother was from Kentucky. Both had lived in Coral Gables, Florida, as teens. Not only did they live in the same town, they also were the same age and went to the same school. Oddly enough, they never met until I was at Coker.

The Dolan's were lovers of art, and all sorts of eclectic knick knacks. This was apparent by the amazing *and* amusing furnishings in their home. One year, at a birthday dinner given for Mrs. Dolan and me, they unveiled an antique portrait of a very cheeky and slightly tipsy looking older woman with a furry beast of a stole hanging around her neck. They christened the piece of work, "A portrait of Mary Helen." My namesake proudly hung in the main dinning room and was quite the topic of conversation at the many family dinner parties.

I will never forget the laugh we had one night, as I came tearing up the stairs of the Dolan home, shouting about the UFO I had just seen. They accepted that I was a bit on the "odd" side, and sat back, sipping gin and tonics with great amusement, as I recounted the mesmerising encounter. I had been driving across town to meet them for dinner when a huge red disc went soaring overhead. I nearly crashed the car as all of the lights along the street and inside of the houses went black, just as the UFO raced by at top speed. I was excited and terrified! I truly believed that I had just witnessed extraterrestrial activities over our little town. What I didn't know at the time was that the top of a generator at the nuclear plant across the lake had overheated and shot off like a rocket in the night sky. I got great mileage out of that story at school the next day, stretching it out to the last minute, before telling what had actually happened.

Crime and Punishment

My adopted family became very much a part of my life. They were there when I was to experience an extremely difficult life lesson, about compassion, truth and justice. One of my new found friends, that third year of college, was a Carolina beauty named Amy. We had met at a popular hangout in town, and we often met up there for a night out on the tiles. The girls from my college would frequent this bar every Tuesday because it was ladies night, and all of the guys from the surrounding schools would come to check out the "talent" as we danced the night away.

One night, I was out on the dance floor when in walked Amy, on the arm of a guy I had never seen her with before. Amy was a few years older than me, and the guy she was with looked to be in his late thirties. She came straight over to say hello and have a quick chat. We giggled and checked out this guy before she went back to her table. This was a first date by her account, and they only stayed for one drink because she said they had other plans. Amy waved goodbye, saying that she'd buzz me the next day and we'd catch up next week.

That night, I went home and had a very disturbed sleep. I had a dream that my Grandmother Grace, my father's mother, had passed away. When my folks called the following day to give me the news, as always, I was anything but surprised. I packed my bags and headed home for the funeral. I was in Virginia with my family for about a week before returning to Hartsville. I went straight over to my home away from home at the Dolan's, where I was filled in on all of the news from the week. The big story had been the brutal murder of my friend Amy.

Needless to say, I was horrified, but as the details unravelled, I got a sick feeling, realising that I was possibly the last person to see her alive. It turned out that the last time she was seen alive was the night that we had chatted at the night club, when she was on the first date. Her mutilated body was found several days later in an abandoned house in the country. The only glimmer of good news was that they had seemingly found her killer, a man who had apparently stolen Amy's car the night of her murder.

He claimed he had taken the car from the parking lot of a local bar, only *after* finding it abandoned, with the keys in the ignition. He said he knew nothing at all about the whereabouts of the car's owner. He certainly appeared to be guilty. I guess that would have made it an open and shut case, only I had this gnawing feeling that something wasn't quite right.

I rang the local police the following day and told them that I might have some information that would be helpful in Amy's murder investigation. I explained that I had seen her at the time of their last reported sighting and even told them that I would be willing to sketch a picture of the man that I had seen her with. The response I was met with came as a complete shock. *Nobody seemed interested in what I had to say.* I expected to hear back immediately from the police regarding this new information, but instead, it was me who rang, a second time, looking to shed some light on Amy's murder. Once again, no one wanted to know.

I next went to see if Mr. Dolan, being an attorney, could give me any advice. It sounded to him like something strange was going on, and he said he would look into it. A bit of time passed before I heard anything else about the case. It was alarming that nobody ever took me seriously, or perhaps worse, they didn't want me to speak about what I knew.

As fate would have it, someone close to Mr. Dolan was appointed defence attorney when this murder case went to trial. He happened to be someone I knew quite well through the family, and he was also aware that I had tried to give information to the police, to no avail, a week after the murder. The suspect in custody was a black man, possibly in his late twenties, known to be uneducated and somewhat slow mentally.

My acquaintance, his attorney, had the difficult task of attempting to prove this man's innocence or at the very least, sparing him from capital punishment. I was asked to be a witness for the defence in this murder trial. This was a heavy load for a twenty-one year-old, but my conscience wouldn't allow me to say no. I knew, with every ounce of my being, that this man had not committed this crime.

I finally realised what I was actually up against when I received a visit from a detective, just prior to the trial, over a year after the murder had taken place. This man was like something out of a bad dream, for never had I seen such a nightmare in all of my life. A classic hillbilly twang, tobacco-stained teeth, and the sensitivity of a rattlesnake. He came into my home, made a few off-colour jokes, and then wanted to get down to *serious* business. Until the day I die, I will never forget his words:

"We've already got the nigger in jail, that's one less on the street. What do ya' want to go interferin' for?"

At that moment, I knew why this whole thing never sat right with me. Nobody wanted to know what I had to say because the accused was already guilty before being given the chance to be proven innocent. In my naivety, I had actually forgotten that I lived in the South, and while there are *so* many wonderful and loving people there, racism and hatred of African-Americans was still alive and well. I was experiencing first hand the very real face of prejudice and hatred towards black people, of a nature that I thought, or at least hoped, no longer existed. White sheets and burning crosses would have been an appropriate backdrop for my meeting with this detective. I escorted this archaic bigot to the door and told him never to darken my doorstep again. I had to face the harsh reality that the odds of the man in custody receiving a fair trial were slim to none.

A No-Win Situation

Under a beautiful Carolina blue sky, our day in court finally arrived. Despite the sunshine, there was an ominous, dark, feeling in the air. I can still hear the people on the steps shouting things I can't and won't repeat, as all of the participants in Amy's murder trial arrived. I was placed in a room on my own until it was time for me to be called in front of the judge. I remember having to go to the bathroom, and on my way back I asked the guard outside of the courtroom doors how things were going inside. He turned to me and said, "I don't know what this world is coming to. I don't know why they're even giving this nigger a trial. Do you know what they had *my* little girl doing in school? They had her celebrating Martin Luther King's life. Did ya' ever hear such bullshit in alla yer life?"

I just walked away and cried. I cried for his ignorance, and I cried because I was about to face a crowd of people, who were probably just like him.

Finally, it was my turn to go in. All I had to do was explain what I witnessed the last night of Amy's life, and my attempt to inform the police of the man I had seen her with. Things began to go dramatically downhill as I was questioned by the opposing council. I experienced what it feels like to have your character judged by a stranger, in front of a bunch of other strangers, with every possible twist to make *you* look like a liar and a fool. All of this took place in a matter of minutes. Very personal information that I had *never* imagined could ever become public knowledge was laid bare for all to judge and then quickly withdrawn after each of the defence attorney's objections. It's amazing how a jury still hears things, even when a lawyer is forced to withdraw his statement. Even my relationship with the defence attorney was questioned, as his wife, also a friend, sat in the back of the courtroom, shaking her head in disbelief.

I didn't know this man on trial; I didn't know anyone who knew this man, *and* this man had been accused of killing a friend of mine. I had no reason to champion his cause. By all other accounts, the guy seemed guilty.

All I did was tell the truth. And the truth was that the information was wrong about when Amy had last been seen, because I had seen her after the alleged last sighting, and there was absolutely *no mention* made of the man she was with in the bar. I was most likely the last to see her alive, bar her date and her killer, but no-one wanted to know a thing about this "mystery man" or the fact that I would be able to help identify him, or the fact that she had only met him for the first time that night. The man being held behind bars seemed a little too convenient, and while stealing a car is no laughing matter – *it's not murder*.

Somehow, after we moved past the irrelevant stories of my own life, enough had been said for the jury to come back with reasonable doubts. The accused was sentenced to life in prison rather than death. I know that our system is not perfect, and maybe we condemned this man to a fate *worse* than death, but one thing I will never regret is helping to spare the life of a man who was made guilty before having the chance to be proven innocent. Everyone deserves a fair trial, no matter what the colour of their skin.

The reality of the situation is that nobody knows for certain who killed Amy. What we did know was that someone else was with her that night, and for some reason, nobody wanted to know about it. Throughout the time of the trial, I lived first hand with the cruel animal that is prejudice. Not only was I witnessing it because of Amy's death, but afterwards I was repeatedly seeing images and having dreams of being dragged and hung in front of a cheering crowd with foreign accents very different to the Southern drawl. "How strange," I would think. "Why do I keep seeing this man?" Finally, one day, I realised that this man in my dreams and vision was me. I was having consistent and very coherent memories of a life as a black man. How different that life could have been had someone stepped forward and put a stop to the travesty, without fear of being shunned, or of what others would think.

Nearly twenty years later, I'm sure Amy's family is still shocked that I would make the testimony that I did. I feel very deeply for those people and their tremendous loss, and I know that having closure would have at least given some sense of peace in their time of grief, *but at whose expense*? What about the family of the man accused of murder?

Poor and uneducated, his very life seemed to slip through the cracks as "insignificant". I will never forget the phone call from the mother of the accused: she simply called to thank me for speaking up. At least her boy was alive. To me, it wasn't a choice. It was an obligation. The story would have read a lot better in the papers had the case been solved and the accused been given the death penalty. Instead, a man spends the rest of his life in jail, a killer walks free, a woman is dead, and two families will never be the same. There is no justice in this story, none at all. It only tells us we have a long way to go to get the simple lesson; *we must learn to love one another and respect the gift that is life.*

Chapter 11

People are always blaming circumstances for what they are. I do not believe in circumstances. The people who get on in this world are the people who get up and look for the circumstances they want, and if they cannot find them, they make them. **- George Bernard Shaw**

Love at First Bite

The summer before my senior year at Coker, I had remained in Hartsville to work in a local restaurant. I had met a fabulous new friend that I would paint the town red with on a regular basis. Maggs was a free spirit, had a very large personality, and was well travelled for a girl from a small southern town. We had a great time together and went on many adventures that summer. One evening, as I was preparing for another night on the dance floor, Maggs arrived at my door and announced that she had met the guy I would marry, and she demanded that I promise to make her a bridesmaid. She had been out the night before and met a student from the university in Florence, who was tending bar at a hotel for the summer. "Change of plans!" she yelled while I finished getting dressed.

We jumped in her car and drove to Florence to meet my betrothed. I had to give it to her; Ben was cute and friendly with a great smile. We immediately discovered that we shared a common bond. We both loved our food! We would hit the all you can eat buffets, sop up gravy with a big slice of bread and wipe a dinner plate clean. It was love at first sight! We began dating *the very next day* after we met, and due to the fact that I spent most of my time with him rather than out on the town, I managed to keep myself focused and sailed through the last year of college. I graduated with very high marks and a clear plan to move to Charleston, South Carolina, Ben's home, to start my new life.

Doing the Charleston

Getting a job, even with a college degree, isn't as easy as young graduates foolishly think. Ben and I had moved to Charleston with high hopes of landing the perfect job and working for big money. After many interviews in my chosen field, with just as many responses of "Sorry, we need someone with experience", I finally took a job with a franchise company that made signs. I thought I was interviewing to design signs, or at the very least to sell signs, but my new boss had other ideas.

Having a seventh grade education and more business savvy than most I've met, my boss proceeded to tell me that he felt it was his duty to give me a gift that would last me a lifetime. He was going to *allow* me to start at the bottom, and I mean the very bottom; sweeping, mopping and cleaning up after those who actually made the signs. I was less than excited, that as a college graduate, I would be spending my day cleaning up someone else's mess. Reluctantly, I took the job. I really needed the money, and nobody in the fields of communications or graphic design was beating the door down to hire me. This turned out to be one of the best moves I ever made.

Frank and his wife, Teresa, were always kind and respectful as employers but more than that, they took the time to teach me a few of the lessons for success. Lesson number one; learn everyone's job. With that, I swept, I mopped, I made signs, I designed signs and eventually I sold signs. I might not have been the best at any of these jobs, but I tried really hard (that 'ole sparkplug spirit of days gone by). This couple taught me that you don't always have to be the most skilled or the most educated to learn a job and do it well. I also learned that when you accept a position of employment, in order to truly excel, you must treat the place as if it belongs to you. Eventually, a business may belong to you, and you will want your employees to treat it as if their own money, sweat, and tears went in to its creation. I have taken that lesson with me always and use the example every time I interview a potential team member for one of my businesses. I am forever grateful to Frank and Teresa for caring enough to *teach* me rather than just give me a job.

Hit or Miss

One day, I was at work when I got a phone call from Ben. He was working in a mall, not too far from the sign shop where I was employed. His political science degree had afforded him about as many great opportunities as my communications degree had, so he was selling a new product on the market – something that was sure to sweep the nation *once it caught on* – the cellular phone.

He worked from a smallish booth located near the entrance of the mall. He hadn't been there long, when a bunch of high school boys came around, distracting Ben by asking a bunch of questions, pretending to be interested in the phones. He half-heartedly entertained them when suddenly he realised that the keys to his truck were missing. They had been sitting on the countertop, and the group of boys had diverted his attention long enough to steal them. They had obviously watched him drive in and marked their target. As he ran to the car park his worst nightmare came true. The truck was gone!

Ordinarily, this would have been no big deal because his insurance would have covered the theft. You guessed it! There was no coverage on the truck and had not been for a couple of days. His insurance had expired three days earlier and he had been looking for a cheaper policy. He took the chance that *surely* nothing would happen in the few days in between! No truck, no insurance and no money for another vehicle. The panic in his voice when he phoned me was all making sense now. I jumped into my trusty, brown car and went to get him.

That night we tried to figure out what we were going to do. I could hardly sleep, and was infuriated. Not only did these punks have the truck, they also had our house keys, *and* our address, as Ben had left the morning mail on the front seat. Just as a precaution, we had the locks changed that evening. When Ben went to bed, I nailed a big note to the front door that read:

"Don't even think about it... I am on the other side of this door with a 357 Magnum and I know how to use it!"

The scariest part was that the first part of that note was true and the second part wasn't! My boyfriend owned a gun that he used for target practice, and like an idiot, I sat on the stairs until the wee hours of the morning, gun next to me, in front of the door, until I was too tired to stay up any longer. I'm not sure what I thought I was going to do though, since I had never handled a gun in my life, and I'm the sort that would remove a bug from the house and take it outside rather than kill it. When I finally went to bed, I tossed and turned, so irate at the day's events, until out of the blue, it all came to me. The heavens were on the job, and I was told exactly what I was to do the following day.

I got up late the next morning and knew precisely where to find the truck. I said nothing to Ben, and after lunch, I left to go to work. It was then I noticed that something was wrong when I tried to lock the door. Our old key was broken off in the lock. Now, I was fuming! I called work and told them that I was going out on some sales calls for the afternoon. I drove straight over to North Charleston High School. An obvious choice one may think, but the greater Charleston area, with a population of over 350,000, was home to many high schools. I went to the head office and asked if I could speak to the school's principal. I was allowed in and proceeded to tell my story. In my excited state I was talking a mile a minute when the Principal interrupted me. "Hold on there, young lady," he said. "You can't just walk in here accusing one of my students of grand theft! Just how do you know it's one of our kids?" Before I could attempt to explain why I *just knew*, he got a strange look on his face and said,

"Wait just a minute; I think you *are* in the right place."

Apparently, he had received a call from the mother of one of his students, who was concerned that her son had been picked up that morning for school by a friend driving a blue truck. She was certain that the vehicle did not belong to the boy and feared that her son was headed for trouble. She had called to see if her son had even shown up at school. She was familiar with the other boy and also knew that he had quite the reputation for being bad news. It turned out that her son had come to school that day, and the principal had a feeling that the truck would turn up at the end of the school day to collect him. I asked if he would ring the police to have someone on standby at three o'clock. He made the call and then walked with me to the front of the school, where I was going to sit and wait for the police. It was about ten minutes until three when we walked out the door and I let out a shriek, as I watched Ben's truck drive past, pulling over to the side of the school, right next to my own car!

My heart was pounding as the Principal told me to stay calm. He went around to the side of the school and I walked quickly over and jumped into my own car. The music was blaring from the truck when all of a sudden this hoodlum saw the principal walking towards him. I knew that if I let him get away, we would never see the truck again. Just as he put the truck in reverse, I pulled my car directly behind him and he shouted abuse at me. He pulled forward and then realised that we were after him, so he took off across the parking lot, weaving in and out of the parked cars. In true *Dukes of Hazzard* style, I let out a yell, put the pedal to the metal and went tearing across the parking lot before this guy escaped. I managed to get out in front of him and sharply turned, smashing my car into the front of the truck.

The boy jumped out and yelled," You crazy bitch!" and took off running.

By the time the drama had all unfolded, the police arrived. They cornered the little thief in an old house just down the road. He was arrested and taken away, and when the dust settled, I was questioned. I will never forget the look on the officer's face when he asked me,

"Who does this car belong to?"

"Me."

"And just *who* does this truck belong to?"

"Me."

"Let me get this straight. You ran into your own truck, with your own car? *Why?*"

I explained the events of the last twenty-four hours and by the end of the story had two police officers, and a few other witnesses, in absolute stitches! Hey, at least we got the truck back, slightly mangled, but we got it back!

My car was smashed in the front but otherwise driveable, which was lucky for me, as it was soon going to be the very vehicle that saved my life. The funny thing about that car was it seemed to have as many lives as a cat. Two years earlier, Hurricane Hugo had ripped through South Carolina leaving a tremendous amount of destruction in its wake. I had parked my faded brown Toyota Corolla under a huge tree the night before the massive storm in hopes that I might end up with a new car. Instead, my car and my tree were the only ones on the street to survive the tornado which spun off as a result of the hurricane. Every other car and tree on the street was demolished. The Universe had other plans for me and that car, and as always, a great sense of humour.

Stars in My Eyes

It was a dark and stormy night . . . okay, it wasn't really, but I've always wanted to say that! It was actually a very pleasant evening full of excitement and anticipation, because I was going to see one of my favourite bands on a come-back tour in the North Charleston Coliseum. Being an 80's chick, I had loved INXS in their heyday, and was very excited to get the chance to see them live. Ben was away, working in Myrtle Beach, and I was going to the concert on my own. I arrived early, and went to a local hangout to wait for the doors to open. I began chatting to a guy who was also on his own and soon found out that he had actually won his tickets *and* back stage passes on a radio promotion earlier in the week. With a toothy smile, and a bat of the eyelashes, I was now the proud owner of a pass to get behind the scenes, and a chance to meet Michael Hutchence, the lead singer, in person.

We arrived at the venue and were given the VIP treatment at the door. Then we were whisked away to the backstage party that was already in full swing. Much to my delight, there stood Michael Hutchence, greeting people at the door like a politician. He shook my new friend's hand, and then before I knew what hit me, I was scooped up, dipped, and then kissed by this heart throb! He looked me in the eyes, (as best he could under the circumstances), and with a big grin and that fabulous accent said,

"Now, girl, that's the best thing that'll ever happen to you!"

I immediately responded,

"Well, Sir, little do you know – it's the other way around!"

He laughed and said he liked my optimism. I laughed back and said he *owed* me for his arrogance. I then requested that because of his delusions of grandeur, he must play my favourite song and dedicate it to me. I waited all night to see if he would make good on his promise, and just before they finished, he sang.

97

"Don't Change," just for me. I cherish that night and no matter what the opinions, or speculations, on the life and death of Michael Hutchence, I will always remember his cheeky sense of humour and his love of a good laugh. All I know was that his music was such an important part of my youth, and on that glorious night, this star-struck girl had been kissed by an angel *and* his "devil inside," and *that's* the kind of fun I was determined to create in my life.

Rings and Things

The summer of 1991 was an unusual one. I was finally out of school, I had moved to a new city, started working in the real world, and I found myself living with my college sweetheart. We had talked of marriage, but Ben wanted to wait until he could save enough money to buy a ring. We couldn't afford to live independently of one another, so we rented a townhouse and I had to make up stories to my parents that Ben was living at home with his parents. I had become quite accustomed to "stretching the truth", as I had strayed, somewhat, from the rules of life that my folks had given me. It wasn't that they wouldn't handle, or discuss rationally, any and all events of my life; it was *my* own issues with letting them down that prevented me from being 100% honest about my living arrangements, and my life, as a whole.

The last four years had been far, far, away from the fairy tale that I had thought was my birth rite. I was learning that life, and its experiences were forever changing at the drop of a hat, and sometimes these lessons left me feeling pretty good about myself, but more often I was left feeling disillusioned. It's amazing how I felt so sure that I was marriage-material at twenty-one and became focused on getting engaged and wearing the ring of my dreams. Talk about pressure on a man – especially when you get someone with my intensity and drive, focusing on the goal of marriage.

I, of course, dropped numerous hints, as to the "perfect" ring. It had to be this, couldn't be that and I expected no ordinary proposal – it *had* to be unique. I shudder as I think of it now. Poor Ben was a lamb led to the slaughter: young and naïve, with his whole life ahead of him. I know there are no mistakes, and that every circumstance is a learning experience, but this guy had no idea, who, and what, he was getting himself into. Ben was such a lovely person, with a great sense of humour and cheerful disposition. He took the news well when I found my own engagement ring in a fabulous consignment shop in downtown Charleston. We could in no way afford to buy it, but the girls in the shop set up a fund, charging me a small fee, every time I went to "visit" my ring. As one could imagine, that fund was considerably large by the time he finally purchased it.

Ben's family lived on the Intracoastal Waterway, just outside Charleston. They had a dock and a boat and a view like something from a postcard. For a girl from the foothills of Virginia, this place was heaven. We swam, fished, went crabbing and shrimping, and I quickly became addicted to the heavenly dish of mullet and cheese grits. These people took me in as one of their own, and I genuinely felt that I was part of the family. Oyster roasts and corn boils were common occurrences and excuses for the friends in the community to get together on a regular basis. I have to say, this really was a happy time in my life, and I treasure the memories of being a part of their world. There were challenges, of course, as their way of life was dramatically different to what I was accustomed to. Ideas and personalities clashed on the odd occasion, but when the going got tough, and when I needed support, especially in the months that followed my car accident – Ben's family was there for me.

Chapter 12

A thing long expected takes the form of the unexpected when at last, it comes.

- **Mark Twain**

A Knight to Remember

Fear does strange things to people. For my boyfriend, the fear of nearly losing me in a car crash, just before Christmas, prompted him to propose, and that very same fear led me to accept. It was New Year's Eve 1991, when I became engaged to be married to my best friend, Ben. At twenty-one, I had no business entertaining marriage, but at twenty-one, *I knew everything*. No one was going to tell me anything different. And come on, how I could resist the "surprise," of a ring that I was now on a first name basis with. It had been lovingly wrapped in toilet paper and stuffed in Ben's sock until it was produced at the stroke of midnight, as the band played Auld Lang Syne.

I spent the next ten months visiting the wedding band in the jewellers, since Ben's salary had not yet been able to liberate and reunite it with my engagement ring. Is anyone beginning to see the direction my life's priorities were heading? The ring actually became a distraction from the fact that I had turned my back on the instructions and guidance given to me by my guardians, at the time of the accident.

Over the course of the ten-month engagement, there were many times that I second guessed my decision to marry, but I never chose to figure out what was bothering me about the whole arrangement. Looking back now, with a touch more wisdom and experience than available to me at the time, I'm certain that one episode in particular, when I was in college, sealed my fate. What happened on this day wouldn't allow me to back out of a marriage that I knew would never last.

101

When Ben and I were first getting to know one another, I was at a phase in my life when I was making a lot of bargains with God. A new phenomenon was sweeping the media throughout my college years. A very scary, seemingly incurable disease called AIDS had everyone in a panic. Most of my friends were beginning to become sexually active, experimenting with different methods of protection or, more often not, – making it a very stressful time for many people. Protection, in the past, had simply meant making an effort not to get pregnant.

The lack of solid information available about AIDS, and HIV, meant that anyone exposed could only expect certain death. Remember, a lot of people at the time were under the impression that a mere kiss could be the kiss of death. The common perception at the time was that death from AIDS meant a painful and horrific demise, not to mention the terrible shame brought upon oneself and the family.

When I met Ben, I had spent the last three years of college, quietly terrified that I had contracted this dreaded disease when I was raped. This was the *real* damage caused by the event. I had handled the ins-and-outs of the emotional aspect of the attack like a champ. It was the hypochondriac in me that had suffered the biggest blow. Photos of me between 1987 and 1991 show how my weight went from 125 lbs. to 160 lbs. during the course of my college career. The style of the time meant that the size of my body was keeping up with the ever increasing size of my hair! Far surpassing "the Freshman 15", I now realise that subconsciously I was allowing myself to put on weight, because people with AIDS didn't get fat – they got skinnier as the disease progressed. I can actually remember standing in front of the mirror telling myself that I must be fine, because my jeans were getting tighter. I finally worked up the courage to go and get an AIDS test, the same summer that I met Ben.

At the time, it was one of the most frightening things I had ever done. What would I do if it was positive? What would I tell my parents? They didn't even know what had happened to me three years ago. Then there was the issue that you could still have the disease without testing positive for up to ten years! I was absolutely petrified! I tested negative, but didn't celebrate just yet, as in my mind, I still had a few years to go before I was off the hook. I remember the day well, sitting on the bed in my apartment, telling God that if Ben would just accept me like I was, I would stay with him forever. I told God that if I could just be okay, I would *never* do anything wrong again. It makes me laugh, to think about how foolish I was!

I had told Ben on the phone that there was something very serious I needed to discuss with him. He was as white as a ghost when he arrived at my place. God only knows what he was expecting to hear that day. I proceeded to dish out the dirt on myself – every bit of it. As I cried, Ben just held my hand. When I was finished blubbering, Ben just started to laugh. Now I was really confused. He looked me in the eyes and said,

"Do you know what I thought you were going to do? I thought you brought me here to break up with me. Who cares about the other stuff, as long as you're okay?"

To this day, this is the most romantic thing that I have ever encountered in my very bizarre love life. It was that day, and those words two years earlier, in spite of new experiences, spiritual growth, and personal development that led me to take my vows with my father on one arm, and Ben's disregard for my past on the other. And *that* is how my wedding day eventually came to pass.

The twenty-fourth of October, 1992, I marched down the aisle, dragging my unsuspecting new husband, into a life that no normal person would find sane or easy. The wedding, itself, was a dream come true. I had always wanted a medieval wedding, a throwback to some past life, no doubt, complete with full regal attire, banners, and a giant chocolate cake in the shape of a castle. There were eighteen in the wedding party including a ring bearer, dressed as Robin Hood, and two flower girls in cone hats and flowing veils. I had visualised my dream wedding gown and my dear friend "Cookie," took on the task of bringing it to life. It was white velvet with a gold and pearl bodice and a giant upright collar that would have fit right in at Buckingham Palace. Yes, I even wore a crown of pearls!

I floated through the church to a song I had chosen when I was only eleven years old. I had seen the movie, "Chariots of Fire", and had decided, on the spot, that the song that accompanied the British sprinter, Harold Abrahams, to Olympic gold victory was to accompany me on my wedding day. I had perfected the march for years in my parent's sitting room, playing the album on high volume, over and over again. I owned this image of my wedding day and had reinforced it with a powerful musical piece that was now manifesting, exactly as planned, eleven years later. I was ready, as I stood at the entrance of the church, to make the walk I had practiced so many times before. At this stage, I believe I had completely blocked out the fact that there was another human being waiting at the end of the aisle, ready to pledge his troth, even though we didn't even know what troth meant.

As I took my father's arm, a wave of panic swept over me, just as it had on the way to the church. I didn't want to do this! How could I leave him standing there? What about the three complete sets of china – everyday, good and holiday – sitting in my parents basement, along with countless pieces of sterling flatware and stems of crystal goblets. What had I done?! How would I return all of the presents? What about the five hundred plus people waiting for me to make my way to the front of the church? What about the roasted pig, and the castle cake, waiting at the country club?

All of the money my parents had spent – the bridal showers, the flowers, the food!! My father looked at me, as if to say, *you don't have to do this,* but instead of backing out, I continued on, committed to seeing this thing through for as long as it was meant to last. I thought I would be sick! How's that for romantic? I would have dropped dead if someone entered into marriage with me with those thoughts in mind. That's *exactly* what I did. I nervously laughed the entire way through the ceremony with Ben – my best friend, my greatest challenge and now my new husband, by my side.

Chapter 13

The oldest wisdom in the world tells us we can consciously unite with the divine while in this body; for this man is really born. If he misses his destiny, Nature is not in a hurry; she will catch him up someday, and compel him to fulfil her secret purpose. - **Sarvepalli Radhakishnan**

A Second Chance at Destiny

Married life was ticking along nicely, at first. When weird things began to happen, Ben actually handled them quite well. One rainy afternoon, I was at home, sitting on my bed, reading a book. This book had been recommended to me by a friend whom I had felt comfortable enough to share part of my accident experience with a few months earlier. The reason she had given me the book was because it told the story of a woman that had also experienced a brush with death, revealing some memories that were very similar to my own.

The distraction of planning a wedding and actually getting married had diverted my attention from the inevitable – *the reality that I must face up to the information I received at the time of my journey beyond life in this world.* I knew that in doing this, it would change the entire way in which I was to live my life. I was also aware that opening up to the enormity of what I had discovered, would not only transform the course of my life, but the key people in it, as well. Honestly, I knew that delving into this issue would be the beginning of the end of my relationship with my new husband. Deep down, I had known this all along, but just hadn't developed the maturity, *or the guts*, to face it.

The clock said 4:03. The only way I can describe what happened next was as if a protective circle of light had been placed around me, and I felt perfectly at peace within this bubble of bliss.

With a whoosh, and that strange, but memorable buzzing noise that had accompanied me during my death experience, I was transported back to that incredible place I had been during my car crash. Lights, colours, sounds, and sensations seemed to envelop me, filling with me with an indescribable joy, that well... I can't describe. This time, I was *surrounded* by "old friends," spiritual companions, instead of just the two that had greeted me before. It looked like the tornado scene from *The Wizard of Oz*, as information in the form of thoughts, words, symbols, and images began flying right through me; I was no longer a solid substance.

Suddenly, I found myself filled with a buzzing sensation, which previously had been just a sound I could hear. All I knew was that this information that I had seen before but chose to ignore was now becoming part of me, integrating and vibrating within my being, along with the consciousness that sometime in my near future, I would become enlightened enough to use it. Once again, I remembered why I had chosen this life and its challenges. I clearly remembered myself in spirit, making the decision to experience this life. I was filled with a deep understanding of what it means to become human and how the Universe and its vast array of spiritual beings are always present, supporting and guiding our every move. The pain and suffering, as well as the joy and elation, that are part of the human condition, once again made perfect sense. Our capacity to evolve, even in one lifetime, to reconnect with the ability to see ourselves as pure energy, manifesting, creating, and healing ourselves, was so evident, that I felt entirely foolish for having forgotten.

I could no longer resist my destiny. Lovingly, but firmly, it was made crystal clear that I was to embark on my life's work – NOW – fulfilling the contract I had agreed upon before entering this incarnation. It was as if my car crash had only been preparation for this day: my true life after death.

Now it all made so much sense; a second look beyond the veil and the privilege of remembering it. My spiritual guardians made certain that this experience was to stick with me. I had spent too long, nearly two years, turning a blind eye to the events of my previous voyage home. This time, there was no escaping it. My perception had just been altered – *again*. My memory was refreshed as to why my thinking, my actions, and my life *must* change. I was being given the formula that would make the work that I was to do in the future effectively powerful.

Just because we have the knowledge to transform our lives does not mean that we always choose to use it. We can literally "see the light," yet make the choice to remain blind. Changing our perceptions and actually doing the work to integrate those new concepts is far more painful than the mediocrity that binds us. This time, I *promised* to embrace what lay ahead.

I knew this would not be the last time I would hear from my guides. I now accepted the help that had always been readily available, and I vowed to listen from that day forward. Armed with wonder, compassion, and a direct line of communication with spirit, I felt the burning desire to use the gifts that had just been bestowed on me. A deal was made; if I looked within, embracing the lessons that every aspect of my personality had to teach me, my abilities to assist the healing process in others would increase. I was to look out for signposts and messengers, taking heed of their direction without fail. Once again, I had been *promised* to be guided in the direction that would ultimately lead me to my life's purpose . . . and I *promised* to follow.

Back on the bed again, I looked over at the clock, and exactly one minute had passed. *One minute!* Unsure of what to do next, I rang my mother and told her what had just happened. Rather than try to explain it away as anything but a divine moment, Mom comforted and reassured me that this was all good – all part of God's plan. She knew that I had been blessed with a very special gift. Indeed, I had, and it was having her as a mother. Faith, not the need for proof, has always guided her life, and this has been her greatest gift to me.

My husband came home that evening, and he could tell by the look on my face that something very big had taken place that day. While he didn't really understand what had taken place, he supported the possibility that something extraordinary was at hand. I was very concerned that he would get spooked, or think that I had turned into some sort of religious fanatic. The next few days were difficult, to say the least. I began to doubt my experience, even making excuses as to why something like this could happen to me. Who was I to think I could have possibly left this earth, returning to the spiritual realm *again*, this time without the trauma of accident or illness?

Slowly, but surely, I made peace with those negative feelings, knowing that they, too, had something to offer. I regained the feeling that life was changing for me in a way that would reveal itself, all in due time. I knew that I was "shifting" when my mother rang the following day to tell me that a very dear family friend had passed away the day before. I dealt with this news in a much different manner than I would have in the past. I became so excited, because I knew exactly what was in store for him, and for the first time, I attached no sadness or negativity to the news of a passing.

Life Changes in a New York Minute

To look at me now, one would never suspect that I had been in a very serious car accident all those years ago. Apart from a quirky head tilt and a posture very unbecoming to a chiropractor, I appear unscathed on the outside. The inside, however, is a different story. I damaged the retina in my left eye, developed a severe hearing loss in my left ear, and sustained quite serious spinal trauma, resulting in very painful symptoms that I will deal with for the rest of my life. I will always be grateful to my adopted family from college, The Dolans, for the introduction to a form of health care that I had never experienced before. The entire Dolan family were avid believers in Chiropractic, and when I injured a shoulder in rowing practice during my senior year in college, they took me to see their chiropractor, Dr. Jim. From that day forward, chiropractic became a part of my healthcare regime.

After my accident, I began to regularly attend Dr. Ross, in attempts to regain my health and my life. My spine had been bashed into the shape of the letter C, and the resulting health problems were immense. Chiropractic is based on the premise that the health and balance of the body depends on a nervous system that is free of interference. This interference occurs when physical, chemical, or emotional stresses cause the vertebrae of the spine to move slightly out of position or to subluxate, resulting in a decrease in normal function within the body's many delicate systems. I had become a walking subluxation, both physically and mentally, with a list of ailments too long for this book, and too many for a young girl of twenty- two.

My chiropractor embarked on the long and difficult task of assisting my body to heal. He gave me a gift that would prove to be just as important as each life enhancing adjustment of my spine. His passion for his work led him to educate me every step of the way, so much so that I woke up one morning, and in my mind I already was a chiropractor. After just having finished four years of college, I wasn't sure how receptive my husband, or my family, would be to the idea of another five years in school, along with over one hundred thousand dollars of investment in this new future.

I went out that morning and made a few sales calls for work. I stopped to have lunch in a restaurant that was close to home, but one I had never before eaten in at lunchtime. I sat at a table on my own and contemplated what I would do. Was this just a passing fancy, or was I ready to commit all of my time and energy, not to mention the loans, to becoming a Doctor of Chiropractic? Just then, I looked over at a man sitting a few tables away from me. He was fiddling with a contraption that looked like a picture of a human body, painted on wood, with little light bulbs strategically placed on different points in the body.

Curiosity got the best of me, so I went over to the man and asked him what the device was used for. In a thick, New York accent, he proceeded to introduce himself and show me the tool he had invented to educate his patients about the impact that interference within the spine had on the function of the systems of the body. I nearly fell over! This man was a chiropractor from New York, who had stopped in for a seafood lunch, taking a break from his long drive home. He talked to me about his many years as a chiropractor with such conviction and passion that I walked out of that restaurant and enrolled in the local technical college for the following semester, in order to get the prerequisite courses necessary for chiropractic school.

Something magical happened that day. It was past lunchtime when this man and I both landed in the same restaurant. The tables were all empty, except for the two of us and a few stragglers at the bar. Funny, that he would have brought this box, a prototype that he had been working on, to lunch. Why that day and why at that time?

Most people bring a book or the newspaper when they are dining alone. I am sure that our paths were meant to cross, to solidify my decision to take my life onwards and upwards to a new career and, more importantly, to a life of service. Even better, heaven had just made good on its first promise to guide me on my journey.

The excitement and "buzz" of making a life-changing decision quickly returned to reality. I will never forget the moment of silence when I rang my parents to tell them the big news. In fairness to them, those poor souls never knew what was going to come out of my mouth each time I phoned home, so the pregnant pause before the "Are you sure?" was a reasonable response, indeed. My prerequisite courses

110

would take nearly two and a half years to complete, as I had little or none of the science subjects necessary to enter the world of healthcare. I look back at this time and can see the grand plan as it unfolded, giving me the tools I would need to assimilate the information and experiences I was to have before and during chiropractic school.

Gentle Reminders

With a new plan of action, I finished my job with the sign company and went to work for some friends who manufactured tee-shirts. This job allowed me to work, as well as attend school, part-time. One day while at work, I was reading a book when no customers were in the shop. I had become very interested in angels after my most recent encounter with my guardians and the spirit realm. I was curious to know exactly what type of beings these friends I had reunited with were. I knew they were my guardians and guides, but were they actually spirits, angels or any of the countless other words I had heard used to describe these unearthly creatures? Had anyone else experienced this? I did what most that begin the journey to a better understanding of the spirit world do; I began to read every book I could get my hands on regarding the subject. Knowing what I had seen, it wasn't difficult to imagine special beings that spent their time helping people out of life's little tough spots. The book I was reading, *Where Angels Walk*, was comprised of firsthand accounts by people who had experienced real, tangible encounters with angelic beings.

A guy, who worked in the back silk screening shirts, came up front to the shop to ask me a question. He saw my book and asked if it was any good. I told him a little bit about its contents and his expression changed, becoming very grim.

"You know, I sure hope that stuff is true" he said, sombrely. "How do we know that some lunatic didn't just make up the Bible and Jesus and all of those other "holy" manuscripts? How does anyone

111

know that the very things we've based our religions on aren't just a load of crap?"

I didn't have an answer for him. I had barely been able to comprehend my own experiences and was too new to the knowledge of the spirit to verbalise my thoughts appropriately. All I was able to say was that I supposed that this was what faith was all about. Not having all of the facts, but enough trust in the wisdom of the Universe to leave the details to the Creator. After he left, I put my book down and proceeded to freak myself out with the prospect of what he had just suggested. Being the daughter of a preacher, I had been raised to believe in the teachings of the Bible. I had always struggled with a lot of its contents, particularly after having spent time in the realm that we dwell in between lives, but overall, I had never really questioned whether its *basic premise* was true or not.

I left work that evening, taking my normal route home. I turned down a country lane, one that I travelled every day. Out of nowhere, a van pulled out directly in front of me. I slammed on the breaks to avoid hitting it. It was nearly dark, and I could see his licence plate by the glow of the tail lights. It read "27 Psalm." The van took off in front of me, and when I got to the long stretch of road that it turned onto, the van was nowhere to be seen. It didn't dawn on me until a few minutes later that I had nearly been hit by a van with the licence tag "27 Psalm," directly after my conversation with my co-worker. I hurried home to look up Psalm 27 in the Bible. To paraphrase, the Psalm dealt completely with having faith in the Lord, fearing nothing or no one.

A nice little coincidence I thought, until the next morning as I was driving to work. I had to pull the car over and catch my breath as I reached the spot where the van had pulled out so quickly in front of me. There was no road, only a tomato field completely lined by a big fence and trees. There was nowhere the van could have been pulling out from, especially without me seeing it first. It wasn't quite dark, the van was white, and he had not been sitting in the middle of or on the side of the road. It was as if it appeared, then disappeared, just as suddenly. This was the first of many experiences which would convince me that somebody *really was* trying to tell me something.

Synchronous events were now occurring on a regular basis. Someone or something was definitely attempting to get my attention. Things began to happen so frequently that I often wondered if it was my active imagination, or was I somehow *willing* these encounters to take place. Doubt slowly turned to wonder, quickly turning to gratitude, as these experiences started to reshape the very way I was conducting my life.

I walked into a grocery store one day, stopping dead in my tracks, as an old man approached me with a very peculiar, yet somehow familiar glint in his eye. He gently took my arm and pulled me closer as he whispered in my ear,

"I know who you are."

I stepped back, and he seemed to look through me as he winked, and said,

"You've been there and back, *haven't you*? Don't worry; you'll soon be able to recognize them, too."

He chuckled and walked on, leaving me absolutely flabbergasted, but strangely comforted. I had just received a message that what was now going on in my life *was* actually happening. No wishing, no willing, no flights of fancy, imagination, or delusions. He was yet another messenger of reassurance that I was on the right path, and he was certainly not to be my last.

Divine Timing

Even though I was technically no longer pursuing art, I still took great pleasure in drawing. One of my best friends from childhood was getting married in Virginia, and my mother and I were hosting her bridesmaid's luncheon. I had decided to make the invitations, and in my usual style, had left it to the last minute to get them printed and into the mail. I was working that afternoon, and after much begging and pleading, convinced my boss to let me leave thirty minutes early to get to the printers.

With fifteen minutes to spare, I jumped in the car and started driving toward the print shop that we used on a regular basis in the business. Instead, I found myself driving in a totally different direction, as if on auto-pilot, landing at a print shop that was out of my way and completely unfamiliar. I pulled in just as the shop was about to close. I handed my work across the desk and they graciously agreed to copy my invitations while I waited. The shop attendant was in the back when her final customer of the day came through the door.

A very nervous looking man, in a maintenance uniform, walked up to the desk. He clutched to his chest a book with a piece of paper hanging from it. The shop attendant came up to the front and asked if she could help him. I listened to him attempt to explain his unusual printing request as the slightly confused lady listened patiently. Apparently, the man's father had just passed away very unexpectedly. He struggled through tears as he produced the piece of paper that had been tucked away in his book, explaining that this was a portion of his father's eulogy. He wanted to have the final words superimposed onto a copy of a picture in his book. He looked as if he had been dealt his final blow, as he was told that she wouldn't be able to help him, and that he would have to look elsewhere.

The man hung his head and went for the door. I asked him if I could have a look at the project. I immediately knew how and where it could be done. This guy had been through so much already, so I asked him if he would allow me to do it for him. A little more than puzzled, he looked at me as if to say, "Who are you and why do you want to help

114

me?" I just smiled, took his name and work details, sending him on his way. The next day, I went to the print shop that I would ordinarily use and explained the situation. The lady helping me was obviously ready to leave, complaining of a terrible headache the whole time I was there, in hopes that I would leave it for another day. I was going nowhere, so she begrudgingly took the picture and the eulogy, and despite her ill temperament, beautifully made the two become one.

The cost of the job amounted to more than fifty dollars. My heart was pounding as she was writing up the ticket because I knew I didn't have fifty dollars to spend. She suddenly stopped and looked up at me.

"You know, I really appreciate why you are doing this. Believe it or not, this has helped me. Not only is my headache gone, but my faith that there really are good people in this world seems to have returned. Thank you."

She handed me the bill, but instead of the fifty dollars I had been quoted, the final figure was missing a zero, making the total five dollars.

"Are you sure?" I said, gratefully.

She smiled, shook my hand and pointed to the door.

I went to a craft store and found a beautiful frame that was on sale. In total, the entire job cost less than ten dollars. I wanted to get the picture straight to the man. I went to the apartment complex where he worked because I knew he would be anxious to get the picture in the mail. He was sending it to his mother, who was not coping well with the sudden loss of her husband.

I arrived in the pouring rain, and carefully brought this special gift into the office. I will never forget the look on this man's face as he walked into the office and saw me standing there. He spoke quietly, reverent of the moment, and told me that he had called his sister the night before to tell her of the evening's strange events. He told her that he had gone to a print shop that he had never been to prior to that day, and one that was completely out of his way. A complete stranger had taken his picture and his father's eulogy, and had walked out, leaving him speechless. He said that he felt like an angel had come into his life to help him through this difficult time. Anyone who knows me knows that I'm no angel! I am simply a person who believes that any of us who are willing can be used to help others see the beauty and miracle that is *life*.

Most people, if they think hard enough, can identify with the feeling of being compelled to commit an act of kindness towards another, even when it doesn't seem to make sense at the time. When I showed this man the picture, he began to cry and hugged me so hard I thought I would break. He fumbled for his wallet, trying to shove money into my hand. I was pleased to tell him that several earth angels had made this gift possible and there was no payment required. I thanked him for allowing me to help and left, knowing that our paths had crossed simply to allow each of us to experience the joys of both giving and receiving.

Nailed for Speeding

As I developed a trust and respect, for the voice of guidance I had become accustomed to hearing, I found that not only was it my job to give help, but also to be on the receiving end as well. My husband had been working away from home for a week. He came home for a night and was to return to Myrtle Beach the following morning. When he went to leave, he discovered that there was a nail in the tyre of his truck. We swapped cars so that I could take the truck in and have the puncture repaired. I headed out for the tyre store that morning, driving very slowly, in fear that I might have a blow-out at any minute.

I approached a stop sign when I saw a highway trooper coming towards me. He was on a road that was sort of at an angle to the one I

116

was on, possibly using the speed radar on the car that was going down my road in the opposite direction. I had been coming up to a stop sign with a nail in my tyre, so when he pulled me over for going 59 mph, I knew he was mistaken. With his lights flashing and siren blaring, I pulled over and waited. I immediately challenged his accusation, explaining the whole situation, including my extreme caution due to the puncture in my tyre. He gave me the ticket anyway and said that he would be checking my driving record. I was really upset as he drove away because I knew that I hadn't done anything wrong.

When my date for traffic court came, I was in a real bind because there was no-one to cover for me at work. I called the trooper's office to see if there was any way that I could settle the matter without going to court. I was put on hold, and the next voice I heard was that of the officer who had given me the ticket.

"Oh yes . . . it's you. Hold on while I find your ticket."

I could hear him flipping through the tickets; by the sounds of it, he'd been busy!

"That's interesting," he said, smugly.

"There's a note stapled to your ticket saying not to charge you with anything. Do you know somebody here?"

"No sir, I don't,"

He also told me that he had received a call that morning from a woman, telling him to drop the ticket against me.

"Who was it?" I asked in total confusion.

He said she never identified herself and then hung up the phone after making the request.

"Well," he laughed.

"Somebody out there really doesn't want you to get charged with this speeding ticket. Far be it from me to go against the powers that be."

I sat, stunned, on the other end of the phone. He had no idea just how true that statement was! He dropped the charges and told me it was my lucky day. I was beginning to understand the true nature of reaping what we sow.

Tea for Tumour

Several months after my wedding, I was in the shower one morning, and came across a lump in my breast. It was quite by accident that I happened to feel it at all, discovering it while doing a routine wash, not a self-examination. I was only in my early twenties and the concept of breast cancer wasn't a part of my reality. Several trips to the doctor and a mammogram later, it was decided that I had a tumour that would have to be removed. Now, for the average pseudo-hypochondriac, this would have been earth-shattering news. For me, something happened that day. I went from someone that had practised using illness for personal gain, be it to escape stressful situations or to gain sympathy, to someone committed to healing herself.

Overnight, I became obsessed with alternative healing, deciding that I would find some way to take care of things myself. I was beginning to focus on the possibilities, not the drama, of what this illness had to offer. This was a definite change from my pre-accident personality. For the very first time in my life, the concept of self-created illness was becoming my new perception of reality. Rather than scaring me to death, this new challenge *awakened me to life*.

Ben was working for the Department of Agriculture, tending to strange looking plants and super-sized veggies. It was an interesting enough job for the time being, but not what he aspired to do permanently. For Ben, that was the great unknown. It was a quality that used to really annoy me, no goals or plans; no vision. *Or so I thought*. In my naivety, I never realised that he was simply doing something that it would take me years to comprehend. *He was living in the present.* Enjoying being a twenty-two year old newlywed that spent his days off waterskiing or fishing, not struggling with the burden of how he was going to save the world or amass his fortune. He didn't over think or stress himself out. He simply lived for the moment. Really, what better time to do that? There were absolutely no other commitments, like children, a mortgage or a high pressure job. It was exactly the time to perfect the skill of *living in the Now*. What a wonderful and completely unappreciated ability he had. As for me, he was exactly where he needed to be at precisely the right time, especially for the next challenge I would face in learning about the healing process.

I was visiting Ben one day for lunch, as I often did, when I had the good fortune to meet one of the scientists that worked at the facility. He had a wonderful accent, Dutch, I think, and it was enough to make me listen to him, no matter what he had to say! But lucky for me, that accent told a story that was well worth my time and attention. This man had come across some information within the department about a concoction made of four fairly common herbs, alleged to have amazing results with cancer. *Coincidentally*, we got into a discussion about this "cancer tea", because he had just returned from overseas, where he had successfully used the potion on his father.

A most interesting topic for him to casually bring up to a girl just diagnosed with a breast tumour, I asked how I could get my hands on the stuff. He said it wasn't quite as easy as running down to the local supermarket and buying it off the shelf. The four herbs had to be steeped in stainless steel for fifteen hours and *nothing* but stainless steel could touch it in the process. It had to be bottled in dark glass and used immediately, as it had no preservatives, and it was only beneficial when fresh.

My first question was how come everyone didn't know about this? If it was so successful, why wasn't the government using this to treat the multitude of cancer patients in America? He laughed, recognising that my age and lack of life experience had never led me to question the motives of the government and the power of the almighty dollar. I was shocked as he proceeded to explain that cancer was an enormous money maker, and it would not be in the interest of the pharmaceutical companies or their investors to *ever* find a proper cure for the disease. I was never one for conspiracy theories, but I was mesmerised at the concepts this doctor was introducing to me.

It was much later before I fully grasped the idea that people were responsible for their own illnesses. Therefore, people must also be responsible for isolating the causes, making peace with them, then resolving the physical manifestations of these issues. *On this day, I was simply a girl with a lump in her breast, looking for a miracle, and this guy had just answered my prayers.*

I was told that there was a shop in downtown Charleston that sold the herbs that I was looking for. I went straight down that afternoon and was greeted at the door by the cheeriest and most approachable Jamaican guy. His captivating accent made me temporarily forget why I was actually there, as he bounced his way through the shop. Everything was "Eyrie" and 'No worries, mon," and he put me instantly at ease. I was beginning to wonder, just what sort of "herb" this scientist had sent me in to get!

When I explained my story, the guy chuckled, saying,

"Relax, no worries, mon, we have de erbs for de cancer tea. You should see what it does for de AIDS, mon."

"AIDS?? Did he just say AIDS??"

My heart began to pound at the sound of it. My mind shot instantaneously back to the past, and for a moment, I experienced a terror that I *thought* had been completely put to rest. He went on to explain that the combination of these herbs was able to "break down de badness, mon". I have come to understand, years later, that what actually happens is the compound created by these herbs is able to somehow crack and disintegrate the outer shell that surrounds the cancerous cell, much like chemotherapy and radiation, only without harming any healthy cells in the process.[1]

With bags of herbs in hand, a car full of stainless steel utensils, and brown glass bottles, I set off home to start preparations. I looked like a witch toiling over her cauldron for the rest of the night. The next morning, I was a little more than nervous before taking the first swallow of my creation. In true chivalrous fashion, Ben decided that he would drink it as well, for moral support. We hammered back the strange brew and wondered if we were going to feel anything straight away. It wasn't until that night that the fun began.

What the tea actually does is take the body through an intense detoxification. The system goes from acidic to alkaline in a very short period of time - literally starving the cancerous cells - creating all sorts of interesting reactions! I must have peed fifty times that first day. I can't remember which one of us actually wet the bed that night, *but one of us did*. The dreams were vivid and frequent. We sweat; oh, how we sweat! We spewed up mucous, and worst of all, we stank to high heavens! Our breath and our body odour were embarrassing, but we figured that something good must be happening – and sure enough, it was. Three weeks later, I went for my pre-op check-up. My four centimetre lump was nowhere to be seen.

"Impossible," the doctor huffed.

After a few more attempts to locate the tumour, he decided that maybe they would do a little exploratory surgery, *just to be sure*. I attempted to tell him about the tea, but his hand went up and I was silenced before I could even finish my sentence. I smiled, shook that same hand, and bid him good day. That was the last I ever saw of him - or the tumour.

121

I have often wondered, over the years, how I managed to rid myself of this disease without the working knowledge of health and healing that I have today. I assist sick people every day, pinpointing the time and location where they left part of themselves behind to fester in grief, bitterness, or disappointment. Locating that point in time and space, releasing the part of the spirit that has been held hostage there, is an integral part of the healing process. How is it that I managed to heal myself without knowing this?

I have come to realise that just as there are many roads to heaven, *there are just as many ways to heal.* It all depends on the occasion, and the circumstances, and most importantly, **where** the person is on their journey. Spirit would never leave us without the means to repair ourselves, if that's what we truly wish to achieve. While I didn't have the same understanding I have today, I had something equally as powerful. I had the *time*, and the *energy*, as well as the *love, support* and *undivided attention* of my husband. We laughed and loved our way through this challenge, which in the end seemed more like an adventure as opposed to a battle. In our ignorance to the complexity of healing the body, we completely surrendered and let nature take its course. It was an invaluable lesson for us both, and it ultimately led us towards our next destination.

Mojo in the Dojo

From the time of the accident, I had struggled with a complete lack of mobility and flexibility in every square inch of my body. I had been told that due to the damage to my pelvis and lower spine, I would have great difficulty with pregnancy and childbirth. I couldn't have cared less, because at the time, children were at the very bottom of my list of aspirations. It's not that I didn't love children; I had been a babysitter for my entire youth and had worked with kids in the church for years. In my own mind, I was still a kid at heart and had no desire to be a mother in the foreseeable future. There was also the problem of sex with my husband. I can only imagine how *exciting* it was to share a bed with me. I moved with the agility of a tortoise and had lost any suppleness I had prior to the accident. But God loves a "tryer", so by God, I tried. It was terribly frustrating for us both, so I figured I would check in to something that could help improve my dexterity.

A friend had told me about how great Kung Fu was for flexibility, strength and concentration.

"Are you kidding?" I sneered. "I can barely tie my own shoes and you want me to break concrete blocks with my forehead?"

I would soon find out that I couldn't have been more wrong, and my complete lack of knowledge as to the basic premise of Kung Fu was telling on me. I went to a dojo not far from where we lived and met its most remarkable owner. Apart from being an absolutely fine-looking thing, he was interesting, knowledgeable about all things alternative and very serious about his martial arts.

Over a bright green vitamin-enhanced health shake, we discussed my story and what it was I wanted to accomplish with my body. After listening patiently to what, by now, was a fairly well-rehearsed epic saga, he gently let me know that there was no way he would allow me to join his Kung Fu class without first completing a year of Tai Chi.

"Tai what?" I said, showing just what a novice I really was.

"Tai Chi," he replied, enduring my complete ignorance about his passion.

"Is that some kind of supplement?" I asked.

He laughed and began to explain to me why Tai Chi would be so important in re-centring my body. I had no idea that it was my mind that he was really planning to reshape. The body changes would simply be a pleasant side effect.

123

The time spent in that little dojo over the next year or two was crucial in changing the way I would create my future. I learned the art of meditation and eventually went from the immature girl that giggled and disrupted the rest of the class to using the time to switch off and centre myself. Not only did I have the pleasure of knowing this man, and his amazing wife and family, but I gained the knowledge he shared so freely with both Ben and myself. He fast-tracked us through what must have taken him a lifetime to acquire. I was hungry for more, and he was there to feed my mind, body and soul.

I am so grateful for the day he handed me a copy of Dan Millman's classic book, *The Way of the Peaceful Warrior*. It was a class requirement and my first formal introduction to metaphysical literature. I devoured the book in one day and, on my teacher's recommendation, began to read everything I could get my hands on in this field. My mind was expanding at an exponential rate, and I was truly in my element. Ben was attending the classes when he could and was interested enough in the subject matter, but I was already beginning to notice the difference between my passion and his interest.

In hindsight, I will admit that my passion was probably more like obsession, as I was trying to bring all of the pieces together. I was on a mission to carry out what my spirit guides had laid before me. This time in my life was dedicated to gathering educational tools, as well as momentum, for what was to come next.

[1] Stories about the tea, its ingredients and how to make it are all described in detail in the forthcoming book *Maria's Dream* to be published by Bookhub Publishing and available at www.bookhub4u.ie

Chapter 14

Bugged About Moving

Though it seemed like an eternity, I finally completed the prerequisite subjects necessary to enter chiropractic school. I had made it through Organic Chemistry and Physics by the proverbial skin of my teeth. An incredible feat for a right-brained, esoteric thinker, who was incapable of balancing her own check book! On the first of October, 1994, it was time for Ben and me to leave the comfort and safety of Charleston and make the move northwest to the mountains of South Carolina. I would say that Ben never thought in a million years that he would land in Spartanburg, so far removed from his coastal home. He was a good sport about it and held fast to the hope that when my schooling was over, we'd be back in good 'ole Charleston again.

Man plans . . . God laughs.

The move to Spartanburg went anything but smoothly. It seemed that there was one horrible challenge after another as we tried to settle into our new life. We packed up our belongings and drove four hours to our new home. We had been there a few weeks earlier, signing the rental agreement on what *appeared* to be a beautiful little house. Appearances can be deceiving though, and our fabulous new home turned out to be a house of horrors!

Apart from a severe dampness issue, the house was teeming from top to bottom with roaches. I don't mean one or two hundred, I

125

mean one or two hundred thousand! They were everywhere, and they politely waited until night time to let us know that they intended to share accommodation with us. I can still feel my skin crawl as I went to unpack my schoolbag, only to be greeted by a militia of bugs, ready to defend their terrain. I knew that some day Ben and I could expect to hear the pitter-patter of little feet, but this was ridiculous! We spent one miserable night in that roach motel, and I'm sure I slept standing up, so I wouldn't be attacked and carried off to the dark recesses of the infested attic above, never to be heard from again.

The landlord was in league with the roaches; less than sympathetic to our situation and totally unwilling to accept responsibility for this chaos. Ben and I ended up spending the next five nights in a hotel. Five nights may as well have been five weeks on our budget. We had met a man who offered to let us move into a townhouse he owned, until we got ourselves sorted out. We moved half of our things to the townhouse, leaving the rest behind in the horrible roach house. We soon realised that the reason the townhouse was free was because the ceiling was badly leaking and ready to cave in. Everything I owned was now either soaking wet or crawling with creatures! We scoured the papers every day, but the economy in the region was doing quite well, and the housing industry was booming, so good houses were like gold dust.

Every morning we looked through the classifieds, and every morning the same few houses were listed; either in less than desirable areas, or nowhere near where we needed to be. On the Thursday night of our first week in Spartanburg, I was at my wits end. I sat in tears and started ranting towards the heavens.

"Enough!" I screamed! "If you want me to do what you've asked me to do, I'm going to need a little help here! We are out of money, out of time and most certainly out of patience! If I see another drop of water or one more cockroach, I'm going to lose it! I want a three bedroom, two bath house, in a good neighbourhood, close to my school, and I want it NOW!"

I went to bed exhausted, frustrated, and damp, not realising that as I slept the Universe was organising my request, down to the last detail. In my angst, I had forgotten the most simple of rules. In order to receive, first one must ask! Had I bothered to ask specifically for what I needed, I could have avoided a lot of hassle. In the end, there was a plan in progress that was far beyond my understanding at the time.

We woke up on the Friday morning and did the usual ritual. We went to the shop and bought the morning paper, only this time, Ben came running back to the truck with a big smile on his face. There was one new house listed: For rent - 3 bed, 2 baths, North side. It was the same rent we had been paying when we lived in Charleston! It turned out that the house was in a great family neighbourhood, within walking distance to my school.

We waited until 8 a.m. to phone the number, and when we did, we found out that we were the fifth call she had received that morning. We went immediately over to her office and begged our case! We explained that we would be long-term renters and would most certainly be her best choice. She agreed, and by the end of the next day, we had everything in the new house. We could have moved in the same day, only we had to unpack everything outside, before bringing it in, to insure that we were not providing a much *nicer* home for the roaches! Every dish and every stitch of clothing had to be washed. We lost so many photographs and books to water damage, but we didn't care! We were finally home, and down to the last wooden floor, and fireplace . . . the Universe had provided exactly what I had requested.

It's all in the Chemistry

After finally settling into my new home, I was able to turn my attention to the real reason I had moved in the first place. I was to start

127

chiropractic school the following Monday. I was excited beyond belief, but Ben and I were also broke beyond belief. We desperately needed the financial aid that came in on the first day of school. However, I got a call from the school that Friday, saying that one of my Organic Chemistry classes had failed to transfer, because the grade was a D and *not* the required C. That grade had been recorded as a D by mistake, but I was sure that I had cleared the misunderstanding with the technical college, and that the grade was changed *before* I left for Spartanburg. No matter who I talked to, no one was willing to take responsibility for knowing anything, and very quickly my dream of starting school was slipping through my fingers. The admissions office at the chiropractic college was able to pull a few strings, getting me into an Organic Chemistry class in a local college that had started six weeks earlier.

Devastated and deflated, I sat, once again, through my worst nightmare – Organic Chemistry. I could not figure out how such an absolute fluke could have taken place, and for what reason I was being forced to start my training as a chiropractor a quarter later than planned. Ben had not found a job, and we could not receive financial aid until I was officially a student at the chiropractic college. We managed to just squeak by for the next two months, going back to a very familiar diet that we had survived on as college students several years earlier. However, the week before I sat my final exams, everything came into focus. *This was all about Jenny.*

Jenny was a girl in my chemistry class. She was plain, not someone would stand out in a crowd and very soft spoken, if she ever spoke at all. I never got to know her, because she never stayed around long enough for anyone to talk to her. One morning, that final week of classes, I woke up and was greeted by "the voice". I had grown accustomed to the unusual events that had dictated my life over the last few years, especially, "the voice". I was given directions to write a letter to Jenny, and I was guided word for word, regarding the specific contents that were to be included. I did as I was told, and couldn't help but wonder, if "the voice" would be on duty to get me through exam day, but there was no such luck!

On the last day of class, I stuck the letter in Jenny's handbag when she wasn't looking. On the following Monday, we arrived in to sit the final exam, and I hoped fervently that it was my last encounter with Chemistry of any sort, ever again. During the exam, I looked over at Jenny, and she gave me the most beautiful smile that seemed to illuminate her entire face. She mouthed "thank you" and returned to her exam paper. I sat the rest of the exam laughing to myself that I thought I had any control over when, and where, the universe was going to direct me. Okay, so I was detoured for three months, and big deal my diet consisted of macaroni and tins of tuna. This wasn't about me . . . *or was it?*

A friend in the class that knew Jenny later told me that she had been going through an extremely hard time with her family. Remember, we lived in the Bible belt, and her parents were very strict, hardcore fundamentalists. Her secret misery gave her away with a constant look of strain and sadness. The contents of the letter I had delivered now made complete sense. The correspondence is not mine to share, as it was a personal dictation to Jenny from Spirit, but the experience is. Being on a mission and attaining goals are very important, but more important than that, is the ability to stop and listen.

Listen with faith and flexibility, knowing that Spirit *always* has a reason. Even if our own plans are put on hold, something far greater may unfold *if we just allow it*. A three month diversion for the sake of a letter from the heavens to a girl in dire need, was worth every extra carbon based molecular structure I had to decipher and memorise. The lesson for me was priceless.

Chapter 15

Tickled Pink

In January of 1995, I walked into Sherman College of Straight Chiropractic, wearing a bright pink top, pink leggings, pink cowboy boots, and big, pink, dangly earrings. With a personality as loud as my outfit, I was determined to make a lasting impression on my teachers and fellow students. Three months had passed since I was supposed to have started school, and now, my big day had finally arrived.

Sherman College was a fascinating place, with a history littered with struggle and strife. It was the kind of environment that attracted a very unique selection of people. Most of the students were mature students, people that had experienced a life change because of chiropractic and had chosen to drop everything to return to school and study their new found passion.

Sherman was the underdog of the chiropractic schools due to its philosophy that chiropractic should not be mixed with any other type of therapy. The education of the patient, and the assessment and adjustment of the vertebrae of the spine, if necessary, is the contribution to a person's health made by a chiropractor. Other types of therapy are valuable, but the "straight" chiropractic philosophy supports the premise that these treatments should be performed by therapists that have specialised in those therapies. At the time I joined the school, graduates were only allowed to practice in fourteen states, due to legalities surrounding the school's unwillingness to conform, or compromise its mission statement. The people that chose to attend this school were there because they wanted the real deal – pure, unadulterated, spine-tingling chiropractic education. The fact that the students had no idea of the future of their ability to practice didn't seem to matter. These were people with conviction, and people with ideas, and lifestyles, that were completely foreign to me.

There were philosophers, doctors, vegetarians, gay couples, married, and single parents. There were those who had obviously come down from the mother ship to study, along with the children of movie stars, famous authors, and representatives of every religious and political organisation under the sun. The students were from all over the country and around the world. I was absolutely in my element, and I thought I would burst with excitement. I was voted in as class president the first day of school – *I'm sure it was the hot pink outfit.* From there, I aspired to be president of the student body as soon as the position became available. As far as I was concerned, heaven was on top of a little, green hill, at a school called Sherman, in the town of Spartanburg, South Carolina.

A few days after school began; Ben and I were walking through the front door of the school when we ran into the school's President and founder. Dr. Thom Gelardi is an amazing personality. A man of vision and unwavering faith when it came to teaching the philosophy of chiropractic, he had a great talent of interjecting "food for thought" into any conversation. On this particular morning, he chose to tell us that many people came to Sherman single and left married, and just as many people came to Sherman married, and left single *or* with a new partner. We laughed nervously and walked away hand in hand. I remember Ben saying that *we* were different, and that would *never* happen to us.

A Whole New World

Chiropractic philosophy started every morning at 7:30 a.m. sharp. I think I would have loved it an awful lot more if it had started at 9:30 sharp. It was a great way to wake up the mind on a good morning, and the cruellest of punishments on a morning after a late night. The walls were painted with things like "A=A" and "As Above so Below As Within so Without." It was a suitable atmosphere for absorbing Ayn Rand's mind-bending book, *The Fountainhead*. The class was *all* about committing things to memory, like the basic premise of chiropractic, the exact definition of a subluxation, and the difference between mechanistic thinking versus a vitalistic approach to life and health. I was seeing the world in a whole different light, and this new way of thinking made absolute sense to me.

I began to see the human form as an incredible vehicle through which to experience life, as opposed to a meat wagon that should only be repaired when broken down. I had a new found respect for my body and all that it was capable of if given the chance to function free of interference. The impact of stress - be it chemical, physical, or emotional, was being presented in a tangible way. It changed the way I was to think about life and health forever. I could now understand why I had been guided to this profession. As a Doctor of Chiropractic, I would be able to contribute to people's lives in such a way that it would empower them with the ability to live at their personal best, whatever that meant for the individual.

I was also learning a new language. This developed my skill to communicate with an infectious enthusiasm that got people excited about their own journeys through life. I was experiencing the *magic* of being human and the gift of our physical structure. I was moving from a body that had discovered its spirit to a spirit realising the potential of its body. It is the latter of the two that has proven to be the

133

most incredible aspect of my work as a healer. Spirit takes on the confines of physical form for growth and understanding. A long time ago, a much better author than I simply stated,

> *"Know thyself".*

My class was small, less than twenty students, so we got to know each other very quickly and became a close knit family. It's hard not to know your neighbour when inevitably you will bear your back side on a regular basis in order to learn how to palpate, or feel, the spine. We all got along well, and it didn't take long for us to know who the real academics, the slackers and the class clowns were going to be. I'll let you guess which category I fell in.

The environment was so different than when I had been in college at the age of eighteen. My goals were more focused; I was now married, and *I* was footing the bill! The tendency to waste time, or not turn up for class, was much less of an issue than it had been in 1987. I did, however, promptly become the one that was sent to negotiate with the teachers for extra time before an exam or any other general requests from my classmates, and usually I was very successful. I took my work seriously, but I was also having more fun than I had ever had in my life. I truly loved being a student again and was absorbing the experience with every ounce of my being.

Danimal

I had developed a wonderful friendship with one of the nicest people I have ever met, a former postal worker named Dan. He and his wife, and their two daughters, had moved from Missouri for Dan to pursue his dream to become a Doctor of Chiropractic. Dan was in his early forties at the time, but by no means was he the oldest student at the school. We had a few in their fifties and sixties as well. Dan was always smiling, had big dimples, and he and I were inseparable.

I loved him dearly, I loved his family, and we became the best of friends throughout our entire time at Sherman. The interesting thing about Dan is he was the first person that I shared my unusual life story with, without being prompted to by Spirit.

Dan became my confidant. He also was a great man to keep me in check. He would get excited right along with me, as each new adventure unfolded, but was a steady rock that always helped me to *keep it real*. It's because of Dan's friendship that I was able to keep all of the wild and wonderful things that happened in perspective, without allowing my ego to take over and ruin the genuine nature in which these events actually occurred. Dan was also a great man for looking after me. Many are the days that Dan bought my lunch when I really couldn't afford it, and every day he kept me filled with iced tea and lemonade. We sat next to each other in nearly every class. How he managed to get the grades he did was remarkable. I never shut up. Not before class, especially not during class and certainly not after class, but he took me in his stride and was genuinely a loyal friend.

Seeing the Light

In our second quarter of school, we moved from the rigor of Philosophy 101, into the more high-spirited classroom of Dr. David Koch. Dr. Koch brought philosophy to a new level for me, and I'm sure for the rest of my classmates. The discussions were lively, the information immense, and he was extremely easy to distract from the day's agenda, if you got him on a subject that fired up his passion. I adored this class. I thought the world of Dr. Koch as a teacher, and later as a friend. I think he got a kick out of my get-up-and-go attitude, and he was a very willing victim of my distractions, because he ultimately knew that we would learn something powerful, no matter what topic of discussion he was thrown into.

One day, we were all sitting in Dr. Koch's class, listening to him tell an amazing story of an old chiropractor that he had known many years earlier. He explained that this old doc seemed to be able to run his hand up the back of a patient without touching them and know what was wrong.

"You know," he said. "He was just sort of special. Kind of like those people that can see light around other people."

I didn't hear another word of the lecture because I was so utterly perplexed by what he had just said. I waited until the end of the class, and Dan and I went up to Dr. Koch.

"Yes, Mary Helen, I saw by your face that I've puzzled you in some way?"

I asked him to repeat the bit about the old doc being special like the people that saw light.

"You know," he replied. "Like the people that see auras."

Now I was really confused. I had heard of an aura before, but generally thought that term was reserved for those schoolmates that ate nothing but green, chanted mantras and had direct contact with their stellar origins. Dr. Koch asked me if I was one of those people.

"Of course not"! I snapped back. "But why did you say like the people that saw light?"

Now he was really amused. "But Mary Helen, that's what auras are!"

Dan was having a fit watching me squirm! Dr. Koch suggested that we pop in to see him for a few minutes between classes.

When we got to his office, there he sat behind the desk, smiling out at me like a Cheshire cat. He, too, was enjoying the opportunity to see me so uneasy! Dan and I stood at the door, and he said,

"Now, talk to me."

In a voice that was much meeker than either Dan or Doc Koch had ever heard come out of my mouth, I asked him if he was trying to

136

tell me that everyone doesn't see light around everyone else. Dr. Koch had this amazing laugh; nothing was sweeter than when he cracked himself up and started to chortle. He was laughing like this now, and his chuckle turned into a big smile when he realised what was going on.

"Mary Helen, how old are you?"

"Twenty-six".

"Are you telling me that you see auras, and in twenty-six years have never discussed this with anyone?"

Well, that was *exactly* what I was trying to tell him. I was now freaking out as my mind retreated to my childhood, when I used to love gazing out the car window, looking at the trees and plant life as we drove along. I was now beginning to realise that the beautiful glow that I saw from the vegetation wasn't something that everyone could see. Honestly, I was never aware that the ability to see the colours surrounding every individual was not a normal part of life for most. I never paid a lot of attention to it, unless I saw something that really intrigued me, or on the flip side, made me feel uneasy. I would lie in bed as a child, avoiding the sandman, entertaining myself by putting my two index fingers together and then slowly pulling them apart, watching the trail of colour and sparks in between them. I now found myself trying to come up with a reasonable explanation as to how I had made it to adulthood without discovering the uniqueness of this gift.

"Dan, what colour is the shirt that Dr. Koch is wearing?" I stammered, attempting to make sense of it all.

"It's white with stripes."

"Now, that's what I see, too."

"Why on earth would I discuss with Dan, or anyone, what colour your shirt is, if I assume that he is seeing the same thing as me? I imagine that when he walks outside, he is seeing the same green grass and the same blue sky that I see. I can honestly say, that I have never thought twice about the glow, or the colours, because I thought we all saw them!"

137

Dan stood there, mouth agape, and Dr. Koch was absolutely delighted to have been a part of this discovery. Neither was able to argue the point, and I think even if they could have, they knew that I had enough to chew on for one afternoon. My mind was blown! This was to be the beginning of a very exciting relationship, full of great stories, tremendous support and the joy of a teacher watching a student blossom, bathed in the light of his wisdom. It was about understanding, and the constant challenge to shift the old paradigm and embrace the endless possibilities that lay ahead.

I'm not so sure Dan was buying the whole aura thing; he never said so, but I think it was all a bit much for him to digest. I, on the other hand, was now plagued with the fact that something that had been a normal part of my entire life, had now been pointed out as unusual. Up until that time, the lights and colours had always seemed to blend into their surroundings. Now they seemed to be on high-voltage, staring me in the face every where I turned. I was surrounded by auras, wondering why in the world everyone couldn't see them.

Something extraordinary was beginning to happen, and I could see it coming. My visions were becoming crystal clear, and I had begun to develop a strange tingling sensation in my hands when I touched people. A few weeks after our conversation with Dr. Koch, Dan and I were sitting in the back of a classroom that was used for reading x-rays. The teacher was at the front of the class, when all of a sudden, I was certain beyond a shadow of a doubt that I could help Dan see an aura. I put my hand on his and felt that funny tingling sensation. I told him to look to his right and tell me what he could see.

"Holy Smokes!" he yelled out, loud enough to stop the lecture.

We went into hysterics because in an instant, after forty-two years of never seeing "the light", he saw it. Dan was amazed, and excited. He was also perfectly content to leave the *weird* stuff to me.

Chapter 16

…When people have light in themselves, it will shine out from them. Then we get to know each other as we walk together in the darkness, without needing to pass our hands over each other's faces or to intrude into each other's hearts. **- Albert Schweitzer**

Feeling the Way

After two terms of retraining the muscles in our upper torsos and arms, using strange exercises that looked like something out of a bad aerobics video, we began to learn the art of palpation. This started with taking a hair from the head and placing it between the pages of a phonebook, then tracing it with the fingertips. We were developing the sensitivity to feel what bones, and muscles, were doing in and around the spine, with the goal that by graduation we could feel a "disturbance in the force" through a concrete block!

There was a day in palpation class which had started out like any other, as we moved from person to person, feeling as many necks as we could get our hands on. I was working on the neck of a girl in the class called Lisa. Poor Lisa was choked with a summer flu that had her temperature up, her nose running, and her two eyes ready to fall out of her head. It was the first week back to school, and she didn't want to take time off so soon in the term, as we were only allowed a limited amount of time off.

I stood behind Lisa, the same as I had with everyone else that morning, when suddenly I noticed something very peculiar. The heat coming from her back was literally burning my stomach.

"That's a wicked fever", I thought to myself, until I realised that this was no ordinary body heat. I looked around to see if anyone was watching. My left hand had begun to get that weird tingling sensation, so I slipped it down to the middle of her back and held it about two or three inches away from her.

All of a sudden, my hand began to shake. Realising that something out of the ordinary was happening; Lisa kept looking forward, and whispered,

"I feel like something is shooting through my body."

I asked if she was okay, because I had absolutely no idea what was happening to either of us. She told me not to move, to just go with it. The rest of the class seemed to carry on around us as if we weren't even in the same room. After two minutes that seemed like two years, my hand stopped shaking, but my heart continued to thump wildly. Lisa turned around and was drenched with sweat. She had a strange look on her face, but the sparkle was back in her eyes.

"Look at me!"

I knew what she was about to say. Her fever had gone, her throat was no longer sore, she had no red eyes . . . no nothing. Speechless, I sat on the bench, and tried to absorb what had just happened. We decided to keep this one to ourselves, as neither of us really knew what to say. Her symptoms didn't return, and I spent the weekend trying to accept the fact that the heavens were continuing to make good on their promise. I had been told that these things would happen when the time was right, and it looked as if that time had arrived.

Lisa had, in fact, felt so well, that she spent the weekend working on her house. She hobbled through the door on Monday morning, after badly damaging her knee while doing some D.I.Y. It was red, swollen, and very painful, causing her to walk with a considerable limp. She pulled me aside and asked if I would try "it" on her knee. I told her I didn't know what "it" was, but I would sure give it a try!

That day after school, with Dan by my side, I propped Lisa's leg on mine, and put my hands around her knee. This time I felt no heat, only that tingling sensation as I moved my hands around her leg. When my left hand went under her knee, we watched wide-eyed as her muscles began to twitch and jump. We heard a loud pop, which I also felt in my hand, and I wasn't even touching her at all! Lisa stood up, and I asked her how the pain was.

"What pain?" she laughed.

She walked with a completely normal stride out the door and down the hallway. Dan and I giggled as we soaked in the atmosphere of the first-aid closet turned healing chambers.

Lisa had told another girl in our class what had happened the previous week, regarding her flu. She asked me if I would give it a go on our friend Naomi. During the ten minute break between classes, Naomi and I went to my private chambers (the first-aid closet), and she explained that she was struggling with the same bug that Lisa had last week.

I put my hands over her throat, and her eyes began to bulge, as she said the pressure felt as if someone was choking her. No one was choking her, and no hands were touching her. At the end of the break, we headed back to class. Disappointed, Naomi said her throat was still very sore, and I figured it must not work on everyone or that maybe the other instances had been a fluke. About five minutes into class, Naomi began to cough violently. She eventually had to go out into the hallway so as not to disrupt the class. A few minutes later, she reappeared and returned to her seat. She looked over at me, smiled, and mouthed the words,

"It's gone!"

Overnight, I had seemingly developed this ability to place my hands on someone or in "their energy field" and facilitate changes.

141

I don't say heal them, because I was quite aware, and had been from day one, that this was not about me. I think that the Universe was trying to show me how I could serve, if I was willing. It seemed a natural progression, and although I didn't yet own the language to adequately explain what was happening, after a lifetime of dreams, "imaginary" friends, visions and several trips beyond the veil, facilitating the healing process was a real possibility. I was well aware that I was being groomed for something other than Chiropractic, and my Guides from the spirit world had told me that this was eventually going to happen. But the preparations for the next leg of my journey were to first take place within the confines of my formal education.

The Politics of Life

Around the same time that these healing sessions were taking place on the sly, something on a much larger scale was happening in the constant drama surrounding Sherman College. The school had been fighting an uphill battle for over twenty-three years, for the right to be accredited by a particular scholastic agency, while being allowed to maintain its mission statement. It may seem like a bunch of fuss over nothing, but in our world, it was the equivalent of selling the school's soul, for the right to remain open.

Recognition by an agency should have had nothing to do with the school's mission statement at all, other than the fact that it was providing a safe and sound education within the limits of the law. Such care had been taken throughout the years, by many wonderful people, to insure that the integrity of our little school remained intact. With all of the ridiculous politics involved, there were several times when Sherman was on the brink of closing its doors.

In January of 1995, we got the news that Sherman would be accredited by this particular agency, without having to make any major changes to the curriculum. This was a tremendous accomplishment for the school, and it looked as if most of the obstacles had been overcome. Unfortunately, a court order, later filed by our previous accrediting agency, almost brought us to our knees again. The court order would mean that students would be unable to receive federal funding for a period of two years. I could probably count on one hand the number of students that were not dependent on federal funding. This would surely be the kiss of death for the college.

A Voice of Reason

I had become friends with the President of the college, and I visited his office regularly for a chat (actually I was always eyeing up his desk, as I fancied myself President of the college some day). I happened to pop in the very afternoon that the news had come in about the funding. As it was explained to me, we were a few steps away from closing down, and I was sworn to secrecy. I felt ill inside. I was sick at the thought of losing what had become my new home, the place that had allowed me to learn, express myself like never before and soar as an individual. I was devastated for all of the other students whose dreams would soon be dashed. I walked out of the office into the sticky Carolina heat and sat at a picnic table and cried. No sooner than the first tears had fallen, I heard in my head that very distinct voice, and listened with great anticipation to what I knew would be an important message from the Universe.

"Get the document, get into your car and drive through the night to Washington, D.C."

"What document?" I asked, out loud, looking around to see if anyone had seen me "talking to myself".

"All will be prepared when you arrive."

"You've got to be kidding me!"

The voice repeated itself without changing its tone. I got up

143

from the table, and went back to the President's office and closed the door behind me.

"What's going on concerning some document?" I asked directly, as a matter of fact.

Apparently, there was a document that the school had spent a lot of time and money, in vain, to get into the right hands at the Department of Education. It outlined why the school should have never been in this situation in the first place. There were forces at work, people involved, trying to unjustly have the school shut down. I briefly explained why I needed this paperwork and finally, a very nervous President produced the goods. My attitude at this point was . . . what in the world do you have to lose?

I went home and waited for Ben to arrive, to tell him that we were going on a road trip that night. Oddly enough, he had been reading *The Celestine Prophecy* and had just come to the part where the main character had made a decision to take a trip, following a series of "coincidences" that involved ancient manuscripts. No more explanation was needed, as he felt that the book seemed to be coming to life.

"Let's go!" he exclaimed.

Just as we were about to pull out of the driveway, in a voice as clear as the first time, I heard "Do not go". Again I yelled, "You've got to be kidding me!" I was disgusted and very confused, but I *knew* that I had better listen.

I hardly slept a wink, milling over the day's events. Should I have gone anyway? What in the world was going on? I was perfectly willing to do as I was told, and risk looking like a fool, but why had the plans been changed at the last minute? I must say that I was devastated, not to mention absolutely furious. Ben had taken it in stride and didn't seem to be as concerned as I was. His snoring throughout the night attested to that.

144

The next morning I got up, and went to class without a clue as to what I would say if asked why I was there. *And then it happened again.* Sitting right in the middle of class, *it freakin' happened again.*

"Are you kidding me?" was again, all I could say. Again, I was conscious that I had just answered this voice out loud, and yes, people were starting to stare.

"Go NOW!" the voice said, and as if I didn't hear it the first time, it said it again.

I called Ben and told him the story. Half an hour later we were on the road.

The Road to Redemption

We made it as far as Richmond, Virginia, where we spent the night at my sister's house. I didn't know what to say to them, because she and her husband knew absolutely nothing about the strange goings on in my life . . . ever. Those were secrets that my folks, and I, had refrained from sharing. I was just *so different* than my brothers and sister, that Mom and Dad felt it was probably best to keep any of my "interesting behaviour" to ourselves. My sister had always known that I was a bit wild and adventurous, so it wasn't that far-fetched that I was simply delivering some documents to Washington for the school. Without divulging too much information, we hit the road very early and made our way through Washington D.C. at morning rush hour.

At nine-thirty that morning, we arrived outside The Department of Education. Bear in mind that this is a government office, and no one is allowed in unless they have an appointment, and are on official business. There were metal detectors at the door and guards on duty. I had absolutely no idea who I needed to see or how I was going to get in there.

We walked through the front door easily enough, and as *fortune* would have it, the desk clerks were changing shifts. I quickly scanned the board with all of the names of the offices and the people working in them. I chose one, and when no one was looking, put my name down as having an appointment with the Director of Secondary Education. We slipped over to the elevator and made our way up to the office. My adrenaline was pumping and I felt like the cameras were rolling and I was the star of a really exciting action adventure!

It seemed that our mission was about to be cut short, when we were told that the director had taken a personal day. We spoke to someone else in the office, and were told, in no uncertain terms, that we had wasted our time. How did we think we were going to speak to anyone without an appointment set up in advance? We were shown the way out, but a gut feeling would not let me leave the building. We snuck back on the elevator and decided to go *straight to the top*. And at the top, we ended up in the office of the Chief of Staff and made a bee-line straight towards the secretary.

We blatantly lied. I was just following orders from above, so I didn't feel too guilty about it. We told her that we were touring Washington and wanted to stop by and thank the Chief of Staff for something wonderful she had done for our school.

She was unaware that she just hadn't done it yet!

We waited for a few minutes, when in walked a beautiful woman, not much older than Ben and I. She had a quick word with her secretary, and then came to greet us with the most welcoming smile. When we got in to the office, we had to confess our real agenda. I tried to keep myself from talking too fast, as I do when I get overly excited. I knew I was on borrowed time and I had to get the severity of our problem across to this woman. She listened intently, with the periodic "Oh, my gosh!" and "You poor things."

She applauded our efforts to deliver this document, and our humble attempt to try and save the school we loved so dearly.

The Chief of Staff was a far cry from the woman downstairs, the one that had sent us packing without a second thought. She took notes and even used a highlighter to mark the important points in the document. She sincerely thanked us for bringing this to her attention and promised that she would do all that she could to help. Her exact words were:

"The day a *student* can't walk in to the Department of Education is the day they need to shut the damn doors."

As we were leaving, we watched her walk out of her office, with our papers in hand, into the office of the Assistant Secretary of the Department. We felt satisfied, and we also knew that our mission was complete.

It all became clear as to why "the voice" had told us to go, and then to wait. If we had gone the first time, we would have arrived in D.C. the day before, only making it as far as the Director of Secondary Education. By waiting to leave the following day, we skipped right past him, because he was off on a personal day, allowing us to get the papers into the hands of the Chief of Staff.

After inquiring about her, we found out that she had only been in the job for about three weeks, hired by the Clinton administration. She was fresh, unscathed by burnout, and she really wanted to make a difference with her work. The following night we arrived back in Spartanburg to be greeted by one flashing light on the answering machine. It was a message from the Chief of Staff, our angel in D.C., telling me to ring her first thing in the morning.

The next day at the college, an assembly had been called to inform the students that things weren't looking good for the school. Just before the President went to address the assembly, I came running in to tell him to wait before he made any announcements. I had just been on the phone with the Chief of Staff, and she had organised a meeting for twelve o'clock the following day, for our President and one other person. Finally, we had a proper audience with the right people.

As a result, the decision to cut federal funding was reduced from two years to six months. That, for us, was doable. The students had to seek alternative funding for half a year, but most everyone was able to be accommodated with short-term alternative funding. There was a bit of griping and moaning, amongst the students because no one really knew *just how close* they had come to having no school at all.

I have never yelled back at "the voice" again for doing things that I don't understand. I was told that all would be in order, and so it was. The courage to do something risky is not the absence of fear, but the presence of faith. My faith in the guidance that I had been promised has never wavered.

Chapter 17

Remember that when you leave this earth, you can take nothing that you have received...but only what you have given; a full heart enriched by honest service, love, sacrifice, and courage.

- St. Francis of Assisi

Dying to Live

Opportunities to facilitate the healing process were presenting themselves at an astounding rate. I was careful never to seek out "subjects" to work on, but always waited for guidance as to where I could be of service. It was such a wonderful buzz, to watch people that were often dealing with very frightening health challenges, miraculously recover and get on with life. I know now that these initial experiences and their success stories were not by accident. They were steadily building my confidence and my willingness to listen to direction from my guides.

The time soon came, though, that I was to learn yet again that the outcomes of these incidents were *not* actually in my control. I was, in fact, serving a higher power that ultimately knew what was best for all concerned. It was easy to fall into the trap of hoping, and praying, that everything would always have a happy ending, but as I soon found out, the happy endings were not always on the personal agenda of the soul I was working with.

I began to see the enormity of how a person's death could have as much or more influence on the growth and understanding of those around them, than the entire life they had just lived. I was being shown that a true facilitator of healing needed to be as clear about the beauty of the death process as they were about the prospect of creating more time for life. At the end of the day, a person can only be healed, if that is what best serves the life path they have chosen.

As I have witnessed on numerous occasions, the clarity and growth that has eluded some for their whole life come together like the pieces of a perfect puzzle at the time of their death. I also know, beyond a shadow of a doubt, that all deaths are perfectly timed, even when they seem to make no sense at all.

I received a phone call one night from a very distressed friend. Her boyfriend's grandmother had been a perfect specimen of what it means to mature rather than age. She was in her seventies, in great physical condition, and was a competitive, synchronized swimmer. Very unexpectedly, she suffered a stroke and fell into a coma. My friend had told the family about me, and as a last resort, they asked if I would work with their loved one. If there was no change, they had decided to "pull the plug" on her life support, rather than see her remain in a vegetative state.

I drove several hours down State, and late that night was brought up to see her after visiting hours, as a "relative" that had come to say her farewells. The room was darkened, and the grandmother looked lifeless, hooked up to all sorts of monitors and machines. I went over to her and placed my hands over her chest. This was quite a remarkable moment for me, as it was the first time I had ever seen the effects of this energy exchange register on a machine. Before I began, her blood pressure was 80/30, and her temperature well below normal.

After a few minutes, her blood pressure began to climb, and her temperature regulated. By the time I had finished, her blood pressure was 130/70 and holding. The next day, my very excited friend rang to tell me that the grandmother had awakened. Later that day, the news I received was absolutely shocking. The doctors were so astonished at her recovery that they decided to open her up and do an exploratory surgery to see exactly what was going on. After the surgery, infection immediately set in, and she died the following day.

I must admit, I had to sit with this for a while, before I got it. Why bother with the healing if she was just going to die anyway? Finally, it hit me. The fact that she died was not the issue. The feelings, emotions, lessons, and growth for those she left behind, by the *way* she died, was the key. I had been there to help create that exact scenario. It was not mine to question whether she lived or died. Obviously, it was in her divine plan not to die from the initial stroke, so that time that she lived after it might raise questions, issues, and a plethora of emotions for her family to explore and deal with. Her parting gift was to create an amazing opportunity for her loved ones to question the very rocks upon which their own spiritual foundations were built.

As far as I'm concerned, she did it with style. Not only did she do this for her family, but for me, as well. I was so grateful to have been invited to her passing, and for the insight and understanding that came with it.

Strangers in the Night

Venturing out to hospitals at odd hours was not uncommon for me in those days. After the last experience with the grandmother, my guides must have felt that I needed a better understanding of what death and dying actually meant. I can recall one occasion where "the voice" now as familiar as my own, awakened me in the middle of the night, telling me where to go, and whom to see.

Late one night, I arrived outside of the hospital room of a once thriving young man that had been involved in a very serious accident. He had been there for some time, comatose, making no notable progress. His family could not bring themselves around to the idea of unplugging his life support and letting him go. I was met at the door by the young man's mother, who simply looked at me and said, "I've been waiting for you."

She was so tired and distraught, facing any parent's most unthinkable challenge; to make the decision to let her child live in a vegetative state or to let him go. She had prayed for help to be sent, believing with all of her heart that Spirit would oblige. So when I arrived outside of her son's door, unannounced, she wasn't the least bit surprised. We had never laid eyes on one another before that moment, but we were kindred spirits, all the same. I smiled at her, saying nothing, and took her by the hand. The two of us stood at the foot of her son's bed and she nodded for me to proceed. We placed our hands together on top of his feet, and a wave of energy that was unlike any I had felt before, seemed to gently move through us both. In a matter of seconds, we heard the machines indicate what we already knew to be true. She cried quietly, and then hugged me, and I walked away in absolute awe of the power of the Universe.

One Howl of a Baby

No sooner than this event had taken place, a good friend of mine had invited me to be present at the birth of her baby. This was a very special occasion, not for the obvious reasons, but because early in the pregnancy, Annie had fallen in the shower and had what appeared to be a miscarriage. She passed a large mass that contained a tiny foetus, and rang me to come to her aid. She was lying on her bed and I placed my hand over her belly and got an unexpected surprise. The unmistakeable vibration of life was still present! We both screamed with delight as we realised that someone very special was on the way.

I had never seen a live birth before, only in films shown in paediatrics courses in school, or photographs in text books. What an honour it was to watch her introduce this precious new soul to the world, and what an appropriate contrast for me after having witnessed several recent deaths. The circle of life was etched onto my heart, and I now was developing an equal appreciation for the splendour of both life *and* death.

In the midst of all of its power and glory, the Universe always keeps its sense of humour. In the excitement of watching my friend give birth, anything I knew about anatomy and physiology went straight out the window. My joy soon turned to horror, as I watched the little head begin to emerge. I saw nothing but hair! Fully expecting to see an adorable, little wrinkled-up baby face, I was watching my dear friend give birth to a werewolf! I didn't know whether to laugh or cry at the sight of this unusual baby, until the midwife turned her, *face up*, announcing the arrival of the perfectly beautiful baby girl!

Pruning a Family Tree

The work I was doing, with the help of my guides, was becoming more diverse and incredible by the day. I was a grateful participant, awe-struck by the mystery and the miracles that life had to offer. With each new challenge, I was conscious of balancing my time between healer, student and wife. Unfortunately, it was in that order. I managed to maintain a fairly even keel between healing and school, but the more that was required of me away from home, the less understanding Ben became. He was looking for his own path. So hard, I'm afraid, that he wasn't listening to the guidance available to him. I had stopped trying to explain what I wanted to do with my life, and he had stopped listening. We still maintained a friendly atmosphere, but our relationship as husband and wife had seen better days.

The next "job" that heaven sent my way was a very trying time for both Ben and I. The time required to see this next mission through was difficult. Despite the toll it took on our already strained marriage, I wouldn't have missed it for the world. I was leaving my life in the hands of Spirit, trusting that all would be well and as always, that everything had its purpose.

There was a great character I knew named Stephen that brought a smile to everyone he met, because he was always smiling. He was the type of personality that would be missed if he wasn't around, so when he hadn't been seen for a few days, I asked around to see if anyone could fill me in on his whereabouts. I was told that his sister, a primary school teacher in her late twenties, had suddenly taken violently ill one day. She had been at school when it happened, and within twenty-four hours, her terrible headache had deteriorated into a coma. It was determined that she had developed encephalitis, but no one could seem to figure out how, or why.

Although I had never met her, I became acutely aware as to why she had become ill, and exactly what needed to be done in order for her to come out of the coma. I was becoming quite adept at "downloading" information about people, sort of like plugging in to their spiritual hard drive and accessing their data. This data allowed me to see into the spirit's agenda and assist in bringing it to fruition. Always, of course, with the spirit's permission; my role was to lend a hand, *not to interfere.*

I went to the hospital and told Stephen that I had been called to help. He had known me for a long time, but was completely unaware of this aspect of my life. We sat down with his family, and with no hesitation at all, I was given their blessing to do my best. I went into the room and faced what had become a very familiar sight; a beautiful person hooked up to a host of machines, fighting for life. Only this time, Stephen' sister, Jane, looked different to me.

The aura or colour surrounding her was exceptionally vibrant and very much alive, not like what I had seen around a person that was winding down, preparing to take the journey home. She appeared to be in suspended animation, and when I walked over and placed my hands on her, my feeling and intuition for the reason behind her illness was confirmed. I could hear her speaking to me, one soul to another, and in an extremely articulate fashion, she explained *exactly* why she was there.

Her family were very close-knit, and all appearances would suggest that their lives were in order. According to Jane, each of them was at a major crossroads in their lives, some with very serious issues. She went through each of these concerns with me and told how her illness was part of her contractual agreement as a spirit: to be the catalyst of change for her family members.

I was fascinated and blown away. Number one, by the fact that I was having this conversation with a woman in a coma; and number two, at the idea that I was witnessing this soul fulfilling a promise made prior to this incarnation. I asked her if these changes could have been accomplished without her having to take such drastic action, such as going into a coma. She responded that only something as radical as a coma would create the necessary momentum for change that her parents and siblings so desperately needed. I thanked her for allowing me to be a part of this incredible experience, leaving her side to complete *my* role in the process.

I sat down with the family, and as could be expected, was met with nothing short of disbelief, a little bit of amazement, but mostly scepticism. I stressed that Jane had made it quite clear that she had no intention of coming out of her coma until each of them had made real and lasting steps to change, regarding the issues that we had discussed. The only way I could prove to them that this was actually happening was by speaking to each one individually and sharing a few *personal* secrets that Jane had shared with me in order to convince them that I was "for real". *Now they were listening*.

For thirty-four days I went to the hospital and checked in with the family, and with Jane. Not because I had to be there, but because I wanted to be there to support them all. I could hardly dump this kind of information on them, and then leave them hanging out to dry, with no back up. Gradually, each and every one of them made genuine commitments to personal change. Funny enough, it was my friend Stephen that was the last to get himself sorted out. The very day that he did, *Jane woke up*.

She was like a child when she awakened from her self-induced sleep. She had lost so many skills, such as the ability to read, most difficult for one that teaches others to read for a living. Her speech was slow, and her vocabulary very limited, but with time and rehabilitation, the doctors said that she would eventually be able to lead a somewhat normal life again. She was moved to a rehabilitation facility, where she would learn basic life skills *all over again*. The day she settled in to her new room at the treatment centre, I went to visit her there.

I had stayed away from the hospital when she first regained consciousness, because that was a time for her to be with the family that had prayed so hard, and done so much soul searching, to bring about her recovery. I was very curious to meet the girl that had called to my spirit, and speak to her face-to-face. I went to her room and was greeted by her mother with a grateful smile and a big bear hug. We all sat down, and her mother began to explain in very simple words, who I was, and why I was there. Jane responded in a very sluggish, child-like voice and asked,

"Momma, will you leave for a minute?"

Her mother said she would go for a cup of coffee and come back shortly.

The door closed behind her and what happened next still gives me goose bumps to this day. She took my hands, and in a voice as sharp and clear as my own, she said,

"Mary Helen, I want to talk to you now because I know that I probably won't remember this when I am back to normal again. The very first day that you came to see me you put your hands on me. I could feel everything you were doing. It was as if electricity was running through my veins. I thought at first, that it was the machines, but then I realised who you were and why you were there. I knew you could hear me when I was talking to you, and I am so grateful that you helped me to carry out my plan. I just wanted to thank you."

Before I could pick my jaw up off the floor, the door opened and Jane's mother walked in, and whispered,

"Are you all right, Baby?"

In the polar opposite of what I had just witnessed, she responded with a slow and slurred,

"Yeah, Momma."

I sat there, like a deer in headlights, but managed to pull myself together enough to kiss her on the cheek, hug her mother, and fumble my way towards the door. I stood in the hallway, back pinned against the wall, trying not to hyperventilate. I could hardly believe what had just happened.

I never saw her again, but Stephen said that when she spoke about me, she always referred to me as her angel. He would ask her why, and although *he* knew what had taken place, she had absolutely *no recollection* of why she called me that or of any conversation that we had ever had. That moment of lucidity had been for me, not her, as there was no need for her to hold on to those words in order to move forward with her life. The words she spoke meant the world to me, *and made every difference in how I moved forward with mine.*

Chapter 18

I long to accomplish a great and noble task, but it is my chief duty to accomplish small tasks, as if they were great and noble. - **Helen Keller**

Labours of Love

I went to school during the day, and in the evenings, I did work experience several days a week in a chiropractor's office. On the other days, I worked in a local health food shop. A woman in the chiropractic practice where I worked had been plagued with a lifetime of gynaecological problems, including very infrequent menstruation and ovarian cysts. She and her husband had tried on numerous occasions to get pregnant, but were facing the reality that adoption may be the only hope they had for a child.

One particular afternoon, I got the urge, (more like a celestial shove) to help her out. Desperate enough to try anything, she lay down on a table, and I ran my hands over her lower abdomen, feeling that searing heat and tingling sensation in my hands that had now become second nature. A few minutes later, she had a sensation as if something had popped. She said it was very similar to what she had felt when having difficulties with her ovarian cysts. We had a laugh, and never said anything else about it, until I met her in the office a few weeks later. "The voice" spoke and I smiled knowingly as I told her she needed to go and get a pregnancy test. She sneered, in defiance,

"No way! Do you know how many times I've done that and how many times I've been disappointed? Look, the doctor said.... Ah forget it! I'm not going to go!"

"You *really* need to go," I said, emphatically.

The data had been downloaded, the second I set eyes on her, and I *knew* she was pregnant. I finally convinced her to go, and to make a long story short, she's now a mother.

This wasn't the last time I would deal with someone who had been told that children were not in their future. A good childhood friend was passing through a near-by town on business one evening. We caught up over a cup of coffee as she filled me in on the recent dramas in her own life. Endometriosis and cancerous cells in her cervix had left her unable to conceive - according to her doctors. Immediately I was aware that this most definitely was not the case. I gave her a brief rundown on what had been going on in *my* life since we had last seen one another.

Eager to see if I could help, we went back to her hotel room and had a healing session. It was interesting to see her reaction as she could feel something going on inside of her, unsure of what it actually was. When I knew that all was well, I said my goodbyes and didn't see her again for a very long time.

The next time that we met, several years had passed. My friend beamed as she introduced me to her husband, and their two beautiful children.

Pregnant women seemed to be a running theme at the time. I was working late one night in the health food store when I heard the door open. I was doing my homework and before I could see who was there, I heard laboured breathing and moaning. A heavily pregnant lady, a regular in the shop, assured me that she was not about to give birth. The baby had not yet engaged and she wasn't due for a few weeks. She was having extreme difficulty catching her breath, because the baby was sitting so high and was wedged under her ribs. This was not her first pregnancy, and she was a bit of an earthy kind of gal, so I figured she knew what she was talking about. She had been in the shopping centre and because she knew us in the health food store, came in to sit down and take a breather.

The baby was still sitting very high, and sort of looked like something out of the movie *Alien*. I had visions of some creature tearing through her belly and wildly screeching at me, but I was quickly brought back to reality when she began to hyperventilate. I placed my hands on her belly and simply asked,

"May I?"

"By all means", she said, breathlessly.

I began to feel a very sharp pain as my hand began to vibrate; however, she seemed to feel no pain at all. We both watched as the baby dropped down, and the relief on her face was dramatic as she began to take full breaths again. She still had no pain, but said she could feel her pelvis engaging. The baby was coming!

She called her husband to get her bag and meet her at the hospital. She walked straight in with no wait, or prolonged labour, and delivered her new son. Only a few days later, she brought him by the shop so I could meet him. No one in her family knew what had happened, and we shared a little wink, and a smile, at the amazing evening we had spent together.

My ability to facilitate change in another person's biology had taken yet another, interesting twist. I was beginning to see that being a conduit for energy from spirit meant providing the *potential for change*, then allowing nature to take its course.

A Family Affair

As students, we were encouraged to go out in the community and speak to people, as often as possible, about the benefits of chiropractic care. For some, this was a big challenge, talking to complete strangers about how wonderful this form of healthcare was, especially when we weren't yet qualified to deliver the service we were promoting. For me, I had always enjoyed striking up conversations with people I didn't know, so this part of my education was right up my alley.

My friend Dan and I were at lunch at an all-you-can-eat buffet and there was the most beautiful little girl sitting in a high chair at a table next to us. Her mother was preparing her a plate at the food bar, so I went over and started to chat to her. I noticed that she had two plaster casts on her legs and that she was having a bit of trouble talking back to me. When her mother returned, she introduced me to her daughter, Tamara, and explained that she had cerebral palsy and spina bifida.

It was love at first sight. For over an hour, I spoke to her mother about what I did as a chiropractor. She embraced the idea, and asked if her daughter was a candidate for care. I explained to her that, no matter what her condition was, making sure that her nervous system was free of interference was crucial to her ability to live at her fullest potential. I explained that I was not yet in the health centre practicing, but I would refer her to someone that was.

Her mother pulled a photo of Tamara out of her bag and gave it to me. She also said that she knew that someday soon God was going to send someone to help them. How right she was, because the help that they would eventually receive went far beyond Tamara's chiropractic adjustments. I kept that photograph on the dashboard of my car to remind me just how easy it was to talk to people about chiropractic, and how taking the risk to speak to a stranger could open the door to amazing new adventures.

Repossession of Faith

Tamara thrived under the care she was getting in the health centre at Sherman College. On her third birthday, Ben and I decided to go to her home to give her a present. We hadn't been there very long, when there was a knock at the door. A man had come to repossess

162

the family van right then and there. They were struggling to make ends meet and they desperately needed their vehicle to take Tamara back and forth to her countless visits to the doctor. We managed to *talk* the man in to leaving for the time being, but when Ben and I left; we were broken hearted and knew we had to help.

This was a wonderful family. The father was a hard worker, and the mother dedicated all of her time to her children's needs. They were always smiling, even though times were very tough for them. On the drive home, Ben and I came up with a plan. We decided to do an emergency collection from the students and faculty at the school to pay off the debt on the family's van. This wouldn't be an easy task, as the students were right in the middle of the six-month struggle for alternative school funding and everyone was flat broke.

In two days, the students and faculty of this small school managed to come up with over one thousand dollars, enough to clear the debt. No one complained or objected. They just gave from their hearts. The trick now was to get Tamara's very proud family to take the gift. The letter they received read as follows:

To Our Dear Friends:

*We realise that this is going to be a very difficult gift for you to accept. You are hard workers, great people, and full of faith and trust. It is for these reasons that we give you this gift of love. Sometimes it is hard to accept when the help that we have prayed for actually comes knocking at the door. It is then, that we must remember, **it's not up to us how the Universe chooses to answer those prayers**. As sincerely as you have asked for help, we have been called, as sincerely, to offer this help to you. You may never meet a single person that has shared this money, but rest assured, we are your brothers and sisters in spirit. Our only request is that you believe in miracles, in the power of prayer, in Santa Claus, and the Easter Bunny and all of the other*

163

things that we have become too "grown up" to remember.

Thank you for allowing us to share with you, because in doing so, you have allowed each of us to grow, to heal our own wounds, and to take one step closer in realising our potential as the loving and caring spirits that we were created to be.

With love,

From the Sherman College Family

To this day, I still have the thank you letter written by Tamara's family. I kept it, because in their heart-felt expression of gratitude, they had provided me with the chance to embrace the concept that it is equally as important to *receive* the blessings that come into our lives, as it is to *bestow* blessings on others. The students at the school had been given the opportunity to give at a very difficult time in their own lives, when they had little or nothing to spare. It changed the entire tone of the financial struggle that we were all going through. After the thank-you note was read to the student body, what had seemed liked the weight of the world was replaced with an atmosphere of genuine gratitude, to still have the opportunity to be in school, no matter what the cost.

Chapter 19

Let the soul be assured that somewhere in the universe it should rejoin its friend, and it would be content and cheerful *alone*, for a thousand years. **- Ralph Waldo Emerson**

Cracks in our Foundation

So many incredible things had happened since I had started school that I should have had rock solid faith and total belief in what was happening *all around me*. Every time I had a vision, heard "the voice" or felt the vibration of healing energy move through me, it was as if I was feeling it for the very first time. While I was in awe of each and every encounter with the divine, I sometimes struggled with feelings of loneliness and isolation, even questioning if these things had been real at all. I knew in my heart that it was all happening, but I had yet to come across anyone that could genuinely relate, because they were walking in the same or even vaguely similar shoes.

Even Ben was resisting what was occurring, not sure whether to be amazed or a bit frightened of me. I can still hear him yelling, when he happened to wake up one night just in time to witness his first astral projection. It's not every day you catch your wife's spirit leaving her sleeping body. I remember the feeling of being slammed back in to my body because his reaction had startled me so much. I had gotten into the habit of astral travel before going to sleep, because after all of those years, I still didn't like going to bed. It took that long for me to fall asleep; I used the time to work on this skill.

It's not the sort of stuff you go to a marriage counsellor with, I mean really, what would you say?

"Well, I know there is no one else she is seeing, not with a body, anyway. She does leave a lot in the middle of the night, no *literally*, she checks out of her body. I know sometimes the spirits have called her to the hospital to do her wacky stuff, and I guess the talking to the dead is a *little* unnerving, but hey, we all have our problems, right?"

So, we did our best to work through it ourselves. My path seemed so clear, but Ben's path in regards to me was getting cloudier by the day. Just as I felt that he had no understanding as to how to help me, I know that he felt equally as misunderstood by me. I had talked myself to death, trying to *save* him from his growing apathy towards our marriage, and at the same time working with "the voice" of my guides. Really, I was attempting to quell *my own* insecurities. Unfortunately, it would take over a decade, and major changes, to break myself of that "needing to save" thing. The delusion that it is our job to save another from life's inevitable dramas is an awful cross to bear.

In truth, I felt like I was making this journey alone, not with my partner. It was like I was married to a good buddy. I'm sure he was feeling the strain, having married into a little more than he had bargained for. Something we were both too stubborn to see when we were dating was now glaring at us. Was our connection deep enough to survive this strange and exciting trip together? Had we reached the end of our time as a couple? I also wondered if both of us were missing out on the heartfelt passion that comes when two souls are singing from the same hymn sheet.

I had never questioned whether or not I wanted my gifts and the wonders that went with them. I knew that by choosing this path, it was going to push my husband and I further apart, and the chances of the relationship surviving were slim to none. Worst of all, I was beginning to realise that it was a sacrifice *I was willing to make*. I longed for both of us to be happy and fulfilled, but at this stage, neither of us were quite ready to make the break, so we remained in our marriage, continuing to settle for its false state of contentment.

You see, at twenty-six, I had not yet discovered that expecting your life partner to meet and fulfil every single one of your needs is the beginning of the end. In actuality, he had done a fairly decent job accepting what was happening in my life. Just because he didn't understand it all, didn't mean he wasn't *trying* to support me. In fact, I was probably *less* tuned in to the personal challenges he was facing. I was turning to my friends, trying to find a common thread in the mystic tapestry that my life had become, and I resented having to do that. I thought that Ben should be the one I could turn to, when, in fact, he was probably feeling very left out. Our lack of maturity and growth as a couple was catching up with us, rapidly turning into an unbearable frustration.

A Heavenly Messenger

Life took another interesting twist when I attended a chiropractic philosophy seminar in a hotel in North Carolina. I had spent the evening, half-heartedly listening to the ideas that, at this point in my education, had become second nature. I was preoccupied with a sensation that something strange was going to happen. I had grown accustomed to this feeling, because it generally preceded a message from Spirit, but this time, *something was different*.

When the seminar had ended for the night, most of the students and doctors that had attended went into the hotel lounge for a bit of socialising before calling it a day. I sat at a table with a few people I knew, when I noticed a guy that I had never met, but had seen around. He seemed to be very quiet. I caught him looking my way a few times, before he finally spoke. The seat between us was empty, and eventually, he leaned over and whispered,

167

"I need to talk to you later."

Was he confusing me with someone else? If this was a pick up line, it was the lamest one I had ever heard.

"Yeah, okay", I replied, not sure why I had even answered him.

As the crowd began to dwindle, I wasn't sure what was about to happen, but I knew that I had better pay close attention. He asked if I would come up to the room where he was staying so we could talk. Ding! Ding! Ding! Ding! Alarm bells, right? I wasn't falling for that one! However, I looked at him again, and I realised that I was dealing with something and someone on a whole different level.

I went up to his room and walked into what looked liked a living room. There was a couch, a couple of arm chairs, and a mini kitchen. The overhead light was off, and a lamp in the corner dimly lit the room. I was conscious of the pair he was sharing the suite with who were sleeping behind the door of the bedroom, wondering what on earth I was doing there. He sat down on the couch and started to laugh.

"Would you relax? Everything is fine."

I laughed nervously at that and sat down on the edge of the coffee table facing him. The lighting was odd, casting strange shadows around the room, increasing my anxiousness, but in my apprehension, I also found a bizarrely familiar feel to the whole situation. He looked me in the eye and with a very reassuring smile said,

"Now, think!"

Oh, I was thinking all right. I was thinking what kind of a lunatic I must be, to sit staring into the eyes of a complete stranger, who was telling me to relax and think in his hotel room! Then he said it again. This time, his tone was different and out of the blue, it felt as if something was on the tip of my tongue. It was as if I should *know*

168

what he was talking about; a memory of something long forgotten. As I continued to stare at him, the light from the corner lamp made him appear as if he were glowing, nearly translucent, and this stranger was becoming more familiar by the second. He placed his hand in front of me, as if to give me a high five, and held it there, waiting for my response. I slowly lifted my hand, and our palms met.

The surge of power that shot through me, made me feel as if I would be blown off the table and straight through the wall! He had just tripped my circuits, and suddenly, all of my lights were on. I gasped for air as he pulled his hand away, and he fell back into the couch laughing.

"Hello!" he chuckled, through an angelic smile.

My mouth hung open as he launched into a stream questions without taking a single breath.

"How have you been? Tell me everything! How did it work out with the family situation you picked? You've got brothers and a sister, right? What's it like where you grew up? I want to hear it ALL!"

You could have knocked me over with a feather! I was talking face-to-face with someone from my past; my real past. He was a member of my soul group. The best part was that whatever he had done when he touched my hand, the rush of energy that had coursed through my body had removed any amnesia I had regarding who he was, and I could remember him from the place where we reside, *in between* lives! He was from home, and now he was here, right in the same room!

His eyes sparkled and he seemed to glow from the inside! I was seeing him now as I remembered him in spirit, as opposed to the body he was occupying while here on earth. The face was unfamiliar, but the essence, the life force behind it, was unmistakable. He was one of my actual soul mates.

The love I felt at that moment washed over any pain or hurt that played on my heart, and I just soaked up the power and energy that is created when kindred spirits come together. We laughed and I cried, while filling each other in on our biographies to date. This was a reunion like no other I had ever experienced. When we finally slowed down long enough to catch our breath, he took my hand, and the next words that he spoke are forever in my heart.

*"I know you are wondering why I came to you now. It was actually going to be another fifteen years or so, before we had planned to meet, even though you don't remember that, just yet. I was told that you were having a bit of trouble, that you have doubted whether or not the incredible things that have been going on in your life were genuine. I am here to tell you that **this is very real**. You are following the path that you chose for yourself a very long time ago, and all of these things **are** happening to you, as well as to the people that you are here to help. I was sent now, to tell you this, so you wouldn't lose faith or give up. Stop doubting yourself and trust that you are safe! No matter what appearances may seem, **you are not alone on this voyage**. You are just waking up to who you really are."*

We sat in silence after he spoke, and when I left the room, I felt as confident, and blessed as one could be at five in the morning. My confidence and faith in the unbelievable had been restored. My heart had been recharged, and I had been reminded what it felt like to live and love in the moment. Once again, the Universe had delivered, *as promised*, and I knew that everything was exactly as it should be.

Chapter 20

Spilling the Beans

My mother's sister has always been one of my very favourite people. She is simply one of those individuals that always have something positive to contribute to any conversation, and her bubbly personality and loving nature make her such a pleasure to be around. Auntie Joyce is also a free spirit. Her formal training as a psychologist never caused her to lose interest in the metaphysical. Being open to all possibilities and her ability to listen and council without passing judgement has always been her strong suit. My mother had kept Auntie Joyce up to date with my unusual adventures, so she was well aware of what was going on behind the scenes throughout my entire life.

In the summer of 1996, I got a phone call from Joyce, concerning my grandmother, Elizabeth. Grandmother had moved several years earlier from her home in Kentucky to the house next door to my aunt in Deland, Florida. She was now ninety, and the congestive heart failure that she had so competently managed for the last thirty years was now catching up with her. She had great faith, bold conviction and absolutely no fear of death. However, time was running out for her, and she still had a few loose ends she wanted to tidy up before she made her journey back to Spirit. Grandmother was now on a portable oxygen feed, and her mobility was extremely limited. She was attempting to finish her affairs and also trying to write and record her memoirs. Joyce said that she wasn't interested in attempting to prolong Grandmother's life in any way, but wondered if it would

171

be possible to give her a little "boost", allowing her to comfortably finish the tasks she was trying to complete. I said I would be happy to help if I could, but that there was one little problem. What would we tell her?

"Just tell her the truth," Joyce said. "She can handle it, you'll see."

I thought back to the time Grandmother told me she believed in fairies. I also remembered the no-nonsense woman that used to hold my brother and I in a vice grip when we misbehaved. She was a devout Christian, and frankly, I was a little fearful of telling my secret, of being rejected, and then having to live with the fact that I had disappointed my grandmother. Even though I knew better, I was still nervous.

Ben and I made the ten-hour trip to Florida during my three week summer break from school. Although we didn't realise it at the time, this was to be the final voyage that we would ever take together. It was so awesome to arrive in sunny Florida, to be greeted by the warm hospitality of my beautiful aunt and her fabulous husband, Billy. I hadn't seen Grandmother in over two years, so it was a total shock to see this once vibrant and thriving woman looking so elderly and frail. She was still beautiful though, and her long mane of hair was elegantly wrapped into a perfect bun on the back of her head, just as it had always had been. She had a peace about her, an absolute acceptance that she was going through her death process, and true to form, she was the picture of dignity.

After a reassuring hug and Joyce's trademark *"I'm so proud of you dear heart"*, I went in to talk to Grandmother about the real reason I was there. I wasn't even sure where to begin. How, exactly, do you tell a ninety year-old woman with a colourful and rich history, steeped in a deep belief of Christianity, that her grand- daughter has visions, talks to the dead, has died and come back to life, and now has some weird vibration coming through her hands that seems to help people heal?

I started with, "I know this is going to sound crazy, but . . ." Then I proceeded to pour my heart out for the next hour.

When I finally stopped talking, I looked at Grandmother, smiling back at me, and waited for something like,

"Oh, Mary Helen, you've always had such an active imagination!"

Instead, much to my surprise, she chuckled over her oxygen tubes and said,

"So that's where it went!"

"Hum, Grandmother, that's where *what* went?"

"Garland's gift; you have your grandfather's abilities, dear."

And there I sat, dumbfounded, relieved, and on the edge of my seat to hear more. I asked how in the world I had never heard this before.

"It's simple," she said. "No one in our family knows about it. I promised never to tell, but under the circumstances, I don't think he'd mind now".

Over the course of the evening, this man that I had only known as my dream time companion during my childhood, and from photographs I had seen of him throughout the years, was suddenly coming to life through my grandmother's stories.

It had all started when my grandparents had secretly gotten married, just after college. My grandmother was a teacher, and in those days, a teacher was not allowed to be married, so they took their clandestine vows, never wore wedding rings, and in turn, never took a honeymoon. The time came that my grandfather had a break from medical school, so they decided to take a short camping trip to make up for lost time. They were a young, newlywed couple, and they took to nature to escape the harsh reality that it would be a while before they could actually live together as man and wife.

173

They had gone deep into the woods to look for a spot to set up camp. Grandmother tripped and heard a snap that she prayed was the branch she had just fallen over. Unfortunately, the sound was her ankle breaking, and she cried out in pain as she lay on the ground, waiting for her husband to come to her rescue. She said the next moment changed the way she was to live, forever. She reflected on that memory, with a look in her eyes that one only gets when speaking from the heart about true love. She said that my grandfather looked at her, as if he was struggling with the biggest decision of his life. In fact, he was. He didn't speak, walked over to his ailing wife, and crouched down beside her. He took his two hands and placed one on top and one on bottom of her throbbing ankle. The next thing she knew, a burning sensation shot through her leg, and after a few minutes, my grandfather stood up, offered her his hand and looked into her eyes. She stood with ease, without pain and in total shock.

Not a word was spoken about what had just happened. She knew that this quiet and unassuming man that she had just married never wanted to speak about this part of his life. Grandmother said that she respected what she knew were his wishes, and never mentioned a word to anyone. Now, nearly three quarters of a century later, she was *finally* sharing their secret.

The stories continued to flow from her lips. Some of them even *I* found hard to believe. Apparently, when my grandfather had passed away, friends and strangers came out of the woodwork, secretly sharing the most amazing personal stories with my grandmother. As a doctor, he had worked with so many people down through the years, and she was told how he had actually placed his hands on dying patients and suddenly they miraculously recovered. He had assisted people through the dying process in ways that most doctors could never fathom, gently taking them through the light, especially if they were resisting or afraid.

Grandmother was even told about a time that her husband had been called out after a snowstorm to deliver a baby on a farm in the country. Anyone that knows Kentucky knows about the rolling hills of the Bluegrass State. Apparently, the roads were so bad that my grandfather was unable to get his car over a hill, just across the field from the farmhouse. The farmer recounted to my grandmother that he was watching out the window as Doc Clark was trying to get over the snow-covered hill. He said right before his very eyes, he witnessed the car lift up several feet off the ground, as if it were floating, and gently set down on the other side. The farmer said the Doc skidded up to the front door, just in time to catch the baby.

Now I knew exactly what it felt like to sit in the shoes of someone I was sharing my history with. You want so badly to believe, but it just sounds too far-fetched to be true. I was making mental notes the whole time about patience and compassion for those I would share with in the future. As grandmother continued, I could see her pure delight. She would barely finish one account before launching into another, as if she were afraid that she would forget one of her long kept secrets. Imagine holding on to that kind of information for all of those years. She was like a child, bursting to tell everything she knew, and in her excitement, I was feeling as if I finally belonged!

My gifts were my grandfather's legacy. I had discovered them through my own unique experiences, probably just as he had, but now I was seeing that this wasn't by accident, *or* strictly because of my accident. That had only been a catalyst to awaken my sleeping giant – my heritage, and my birth rite as a light worker on this planet.

As she spoke, I began to recall several accounts of Grandmother's connection to my grandfather, Judge, which had long been forgotten. Now my fears of sharing my story seemed totally unfounded. I had completely forgotten about the time that Grandmother had been driving back to her home after a trip away, when she got an

175

overwhelming sensation that she needed to pull the car over and pray for her husband. Apparently, she prayed until the feeling left her, and later found out, that at that exact moment, my Grandfather's medical practice had been robbed, and he had been held at gunpoint, while the assailants tore the office apart looking for prescription drugs.

There had been another time that Grandmother had been staying at our house; several years after Judge had passed away. Due to fly to Florida the following morning, Grandmother walked into the kitchen, picked up the phone and rang the airline to cancel her flight. We were all sitting around the kitchen table eating our breakfast when she explained that the night before; she had dreamed that she was sitting on the airplane when she looked up, only to see her husband walking down the aisle towards her. He took her by the hand and said,

"Come on, Elizabeth, sweetheart, this is not your flight."

Without a moment's hesitation or a second thought, she cancelled her booking. A flight went down over Florida that day, killing all on board. None of the family can remember if that was the flight she was supposed to be on, but it *was* Florida that she was flying to, and my mother and aunt both remember the incident well. What was outstanding about Grandmother was her complete and utter trust in the message she had been given in that dream. She didn't care if it cost her a little more to take another flight, or if anyone thought her a fool for following a dream. She took her message from beyond quite seriously, and as far as any of us know, it very well may have saved her life.

It's funny how those things had slipped my mind, over the years, when in actuality, Grandmother would have probably found it the easiest out of anyone in the family to relate to my stories of psychic adventures and healing. I laugh now at how ridiculous my fears of telling my little secret were. The chance to share this part of myself with this amazing woman is a gift I will treasure always. Sadly, but

176

with gratitude and a complete sense of closure, I said goodbye. It would be the last time I would see her alive, and the picture of aged beauty and grace is the way I will always see her in my mind.

My parents had just returned from a trip to Ireland, a place both of them dearly loved, and a place that I had dreamed of visiting, from the very first time that I watched *The Quiet Man*, starring John Wayne and Maureen O'Hara, on the one o'clock feature films back in grade school. My mother couldn't wait to hear what had happened with Grandmother. When I told her the news about her father, she sat quietly for a moment and then said,

"You know, that makes an awful lot of sense."

"It does?" I asked, dying to know why!

Mom recounted that when my brother Jon had been about four years old, he had become extremely ill; lifeless, with a sky high temperature that had developed overnight. Grandmother and Judge happened to be visiting them in Virginia at the time. She went back to the bedroom to check on Jon, and found her father, holding his hand a few inches above his head. Later that evening, that same very sick little boy was running around as if nothing had ever happened. Mom said that she had never put two and two together, but now it made so much sense.

She was thrilled to hear all the stories that Grandmother had told me, and was even more excited that I had spent this quality time with her mother. I told mom that she and my dad must get down to Florida in the very near future. I told her that she needed to spend time with Grandmother while she was still able to enjoy the visit. They planned a trip for the early autumn. When they arrived in Florida, they found grandmother to be in good spirits. She had rallied back to a state of health that saw her through another year. She was one tough old bird!

177

Waxing Lyrical

When Ben and I left Deland, I knew that I would never see my grandmother again. We had even discussed me singing at her funeral, whenever that may be; however, she said if singing at the funeral interfered with my schooling, she would haunt me from the spirit world! No better woman, I might add. The prospect of her ability to rattle my cage from beyond was not even worth contemplating. I gave her my word that I would not sing at her funeral if it clashed with school commitments. It was a promise she insisted I make, so I made it, said my farewells, and headed home.

On the drive back to South Carolina, Ben and I stopped in to the old village of St. Augustine, Florida. I was well used to getting readings, or energetic impressions of a place I had never visited before, but this one was a bit on the freaky side. It was uncanny how well knew my way around and had the very distinct feeling that I had been there before.

Ben and I went to a candle shop, where they were dipping people's hands in wax, making sculptures out of the finished products. We dipped our hands in the same position as Michelangelo's "Hand of God Touching Adam." Our two hands touching were gently wrapped and placed in a bag for the trip home. Even with the air- conditioning on, our masterpiece had taken on a twisted form due to the heat, looking nothing like it did at the start of our journey; a prophetic indication of what we had become as a couple and what was to become of us in the not so distant future.

Something Fishy in the Air

Ben and I had become very close over the last year with a group that consisted of three other couples. None of them were aware of our *lack* of marital bliss, so when our friends suggested that they wanted to take us out to celebrate our fourth wedding anniversary, we decided that we would go.

It was October 24th, 1996, and we went out to a Japanese restaurant in Greenville, the next town over. Something strange was in the air (or the sushi) that night. I don't know if the moon was waxing or waning or if the planets were in some sort of wacky alignment, but some outrageous force was at work. By the next morning, Ben and I, as well as two of the three other couples, had broken up *for good*.

Four years, to the day, after we had tied the knot, our knot *and* the thread that it was hanging on, unravelled in a most bizarre fashion. It shocked both Ben and me and everyone that knew us. Because no one had been aware that our troubles had been brewing for quite some time, everyone thought that *I* had just had a little tantrum, and everything would work itself out. It looked as if I had made a spur-of-the-moment decision to abandon my husband and my marriage, and most everyone saw Ben as the victim of my rash behaviour.

It was then that I really learned not to be bothered by what other people think. Rumours flew around at lightning speed that I must be having an affair, or that maybe I was gay. After all, they speculated, I did have a lot of friends that were gay and I certainly knew a lot of married men, so one of them must be true. No mention was made that maybe I had just realised that there was nothing left that could benefit either of us from remaining in this relationship for another day. It was a hard time for both of us. Ben even told me that he didn't realise that we had a problem. It was *that* conversation that made me aware, that as difficult as this time was, leaving this marriage was the right thing to do.

I went out that same week and cut off all of my long blonde hair. (Why do women do that when a relationship ends?). I changed my look and began to go running again. This was something I had not done in years. I found it very difficult at first, as each step felt like someone was knifing me in the back. Eventually, I found my pace and began to focus on reclaiming my state of health, prior to my accident, and my marriage. Ben moved back to his home town, and bar one fifteen minute conversation the following summer, I never saw, or spoke, to him again.

I would have preferred to remain friends, but I realise that this is not possible for everyone. We all deal with disappointment in our own ways, and Ben requested that we not keep in contact, so I have always honoured that request. I have often wondered what became of him, and his family. They were such an important part of that time in my life. I have never wished them anything but love and joy, and I will forever be grateful to Ben for what he taught me and for the precious time that we shared.

Home for the Holidays

I spent that Christmas at home with my parents. I was happy to be there and enjoyed reconnecting with some of my childhood friends. I had no regrets that I was spending my first Christmas in five years without Ben, because I had already moved on. There's one thing about me; when I've made up my mind and committed to change, I always follow through. I am not the type to wallow in "what if" or "if only I had . . ." Reflection on the past, with an objective of learning what changes are necessary to move forward, is a healthy and productive activity. Leaving pieces of yourself behind in what you or others judge as past mistakes is only laying a template for disease to manifest later in life. I had learned this through my own experiences and through the invaluable teachings of medical intuitive and author, Carolyn Myss. She was my author of choice at that time in my life, and the way that I chose to deal with my "issues" was inspired by her words. It all made so much sense. She was eloquently verbalising what I knew to be true in my heart.

No matter what the challenge is that we face today, life goes on tomorrow and the way that we handle yesterday can make, or break us in the future. It is impossible to remain healthy and whole, if part of you is still visiting the phantoms of the past.

Shaking Hands with the Devil

I met a great new friend during that Christmas break, who introduced me to the concept of sitting with myself and embracing my dark side. We became close very quickly, and I had shared with him many of the episodes that were going on in my life. With great interest and reflection, he gently challenged my intentions, asking me to look at what my ego was getting out of all of this. My first instinct was to turn on my heel and leave, but fortunately, I really listened, and took on board what he was saying. He wasn't judging my motives; he was asking me to explore where my ego stood in all of these experiences. It was okay if it made the occasional appearance, the work I was doing with people was incredible. He was teaching me not to fear if my ego was involved in my work, but to embrace the fact that when I saw glimpses of my ego, I needed to listen to why it was present, and what it was trying to show me about myself.

In telling my story to anyone, I had always been so careful not to come across like I thought I was something extraordinary in heaven's eyes. In fact, I often made comments like, "this could happen to anyone" or "I'm sure everyone is capable of doing these things if they really want to." I was constantly attempting to downplay my role in these events, so as not to appear arrogant. I never wanted to give the impression that I didn't think that everyone was gifted and special. In reality, I did not want to be judged, or made to feel as if there *wasn't* something special going on, when I *knew* that there was. I couldn't stand it, when I heard myself making these comments, but it was a

181

habit that I found hard to break. It all went back to the fact that I was asking people to believe something so incredible, that I sometimes questioned whether I actually believed it myself. In short, I did not like the idea of having to defend my calling. The catch was: *No one was asking me to.* The fear that no one would believe me was actually my own fear – that *I* didn't believe me, despite that fact that the Universal truth had *always* backed me up, *as promised.*

My friend had taught me one of the most valuable lessons I have ever learned, and thank God, I stuck around to listen. He had introduced me to what I considered to be one of my worst character flaws, and made me shake hands with it, hear what it had to offer me, and then accept it as a part of who I was.

The concept of shaking hands with your dark side means that you no longer blame other people or circumstances for the state of your physical, emotional and spiritual well-being, or lack thereof. This allows you to accept the fact that certain aspects of your own personality have forged the person that you are today. By embracing what some may perceive as your negative qualities, (in my case, the fear of no one believing my life experiences) you are given the opportunity to experience the need for faith in yourself, regardless of whether others validate you or not.

The best description I have ever come across regarding the value of embracing the fears that we have about our shadow selves is found in a remarkable book called, *The Dark Side of the Light Chasers*, by Debbie Ford. I read this book many years after being taught the concept, and I found her insight, wisdom, and interpretation of this topic to be down-to-earth, honest and refreshing. I was now mastering a new tool which was an essential part of my package. Being free of self-imposed chains would allow me to continue my work, teaching by example, not by theory.

Chapter 21

The hallmark of a divine experience, regardless of what form it takes, is that it gets your attention and leads you to think something out of the ordinary might be happening to you.

- Caroline Myss

Highway Robbery

I returned to school in mid January, 1997, feeling rejuvenated and ready to face the world. I was driving from Virginia; returning to South Carolina when I had to make a pit-stop, just outside of Charlotte, North Carolina. The rest area was large and the building that held the bathrooms was made of brick with no windows. One thing about my father, is no matter how old I get, I am always given a little "pocket cash" every time I leave home after a visit. At the time, it was desperately needed as I was now a twenty-six year old, nearly divorced college student, working several different jobs to make ends meet. I had been driving with the window down a few inches to keep myself awake, and thought nothing about it when I locked the car, leaving my handbag on the front seat. I went into the restroom and literally, just as I was about to sit on the toilet, it was as if a movie was playing in front of my eyes on the door to the stall. As clear as day, I could see an older style, white convertible pulling up next to my car. A guy that looked to be close to my age jumped out of the passenger seat and as quick as a flash, had managed to somehow get my handbag off of the front seat and through the small space left in the window. I shrieked as I went running out the door, barely able to get my trousers back up, just in time to see the same white convertible, driven by a girl, with the guy in the passenger seat that I had just seen in my vision. I ran as

183

fast as I could as they backed out of the space next to my car and stood in front of the car, screaming,

"STOP!!"

The car stopped and the guy looked at me and said with a smirk,

"Can I help you with something?"

" Dude! I know you have my bag in your car and I know that you know that I was in that building so obviously something freaky is going on here! Unless you want to find out just how freaky I can get, you better hand over the bag now. The money in it is all that I have."

Believe it or not, he did. He was so completely shocked by the fact that I knew he had taken the bag he simply handed it over and the girl driving the car looked at me like I had forty heads before she burned rubber and took off.

I always laugh when I recall this story because it reminds of the fact that the

Universe is always looking out for us, and when we're in the zone…wonders never cease. Over the years so many people have asked me,

"If you're so psychic, why don't you know the lottery numbers?"

I have always known that personal gain is not the objective of working with Spirit, but in the case of having something returned that already belongs to me, it sure does come in handy.

Psychic Signposts

Winter quickly came to an end, as it does in South Carolina, and by March, spring was in the air. Spring wasn't the only thing in the air; something new, unlike anything I had ever experienced, began to appear in my vision. I was sitting at home one evening doing some school work, when I caught something out of the corner of my eye. At first I thought I was seeing floaters (little black spots that were always in my visual field) from the damage done to my retina in the car accident. I sat back, closed my eyes and there, in my mind's eye, were three symbols. I didn't recognise them from anywhere.

The first thing that came to mind was Egyptian hieroglyphics. I had limited knowledge of Egyptology, and yet they didn't look like any hieroglyphics I had ever seen. The symbols appeared, one by one, and were flaming orange in colour.

"Flaming, orange symbols? You've got to be joking!"

Either the Universe was once again showing it's never ending sense of humour, or someone out there simply thought I was that stupid that only something as dramatic as flaming symbols would get my attention!

The same three symbols flashed over and over, as if waiting for me to memorize them, or write them down. I studied each one in my mind, and then drew pictures of all three. Once I had noted each of them, the visions stopped.

For the next month or so, I continued to see symbols, only with each encounter a different set of three would appear. Each time I recorded them, and I still had absolutely no idea what they meant. After seven lots of symbols, I was left with what looked like some sort of an alphabet.

I still had no idea why they had turned up, why they were in groups of three, why there were twenty-one in total, or what in the world was going to happen next.[1]

After Ben had moved out, I wanted a housemate to help with

the expenses, as well as for a bit of company. In walked Jo. He was such a character, and his wacky sense of humour made coming home in the evening something to look forward to. We got along famously (as they say in the South), and his energy, as well as his interest in the metaphysical, were a welcome addition to my home. We had such a blast! I couldn't have asked for a better living arrangement. He was always bringing unique and interesting personalities over to the house. When he asked, one day, if I minded if he hosted an evening with a psychic and invite a few friends, I told him to knock himself out.

I had been working that night, so the event was well under way when I arrived home. People were waiting patiently in my sitting room to have their one on one session in the front room with Psychic Suzy. It looked like they were enjoying themselves, and as the evening was wrapping up, Jo knocked on my door and said,

"Hey, she wants to see you."

"Me? Why does she want to see me? Tell her thanks, but I'm sure she's done enough for one night."

"You better go in there," he said. "I think she has something to tell you."

Curiosity got the best of me, and for the first time in my life, I found myself sitting toe-to-toe with a psychic. Ironically, I had never really felt the need. She was a lovely lady (no turbans or big, gold hoop earrings), just an average person you would pass no remarks on if you met her on the street. I was intrigued by her confidence to do readings on the spot for people. Up until this moment, most of my experiences were "sent" to me, and I had never really "read" people, the way she was about to read me. She immediately acknowledged me as a colleague. She said that I was surrounded with help from the heavens, and not only was I clairvoyant, I was also here doing very special work that involved metaphysical healing. Not bad, but nothing that she couldn't have possibly said to anyone else. It wasn't that I doubted her, but nothing really seemed that specific. *That was, until she spoke again.*

"A light switch; I keep seeing a light switch turning on."

"Okay," I said, still unimpressed. "What does that mean?"

"When I see a light switch turning on, it means that you have been shown your destiny," she replied.

She sat quietly and closed her eyes for a moment, and then looked at me and smiled.

"You've been seeing something: symbols of some sort. These are your destiny, and they have something to do with someone you used to be, and somewhere you will be in the near future."

Now, she had my attention. I had told no one, not Jo or even my confidant, Dan, about the visions.

"Eventually," she continued, "you will meet with a circle of twelve. These will be twelve people that are from your distant past. You will recognise each one when you meet, and the work you will do together will move you one step closer to accomplishing your purpose here. This won't be here in America. It's definitely abroad."

When she had finished, I filed the experience away in the back of my mind, impressed that she knew about the symbols, but disappointed, because I knew I was not going abroad any time soon. I was flat broke, and I still had another year to go before I finished school.

---

[1] More information on the origins of these symbols is available in *Gnosis: The Story of How We Begin to Remember* by the Rev. Dr. L. E. Graham published by Book Hub Publishing and Edge Publishers (2009. The book is available from www.bookhub4u.ie and www.edgepublishers.com

Back in the Game

My divorce came through in April 1997. I really had no interest in meeting anyone else because I was finally getting to know myself, independent of the dramas of having an intimate partner. Obviously, the Universe had different ideas for me *and* my independence and decided to shake things up a bit. A new guy was transferred in to my class . . . and I simply couldn't help myself!

Dave was a unique individual. He was originally from Philadelphia, Pennsylvania, and made the twelve-hour drive home nearly every weekend to work in his landscaping business. He had kept it running, even after moving to South Carolina, to help pay his way through school. I had never met anyone like him. He had the tough guy, Philly accent, was of Polish and Italian descent, and had a body that was as finely tuned as the great big pickup truck that he drove.

Dave was ten years my senior, but looked younger and in better shape than most guys half his age. His energy was endless. The funniest part was that we were such an unlikely pair. I was Miss School Spirit, President of the Student Body, the real cheerleader type, and he was like something out of *Rebel without a Cause*. I lived a very public life, always in the middle of everything, while he attended his classes, remaining detached from the social aspect of school and very private in his personal life. For whatever reason, it worked. We had a carefree, no hassle relationship. We were in the gym working out together at five-thirty every morning, his routine, not mine. I can honestly think of nothing worse, but I just pretended that I was *so excited* to be there because I liked him so much!

Over the next few months my body, as well as my self-confidence, transformed. I was experiencing a level of physical and mental well-being that I had never achieved. Everyone noticed, and people got a real kick out of Dave and me. When we first began to date, I worked up the nerve and picked an opportune moment to tell him about *the real me.*

He laughed, and said,

"That's cool M.H., ya' gotta do what ya' gotta do."

That was it. No other response. It wasn't that he didn't care about my spiritual side, but he was a man with a rock solid agenda for his own life, so in the grand scheme of things, as far as he figured, it really had very little to do with him. I actually found that very attractive. He said he liked his girls a little freaky, and freaky is exactly what he got! I felt free to do what I needed to do. This relationship had been handed to me by a divine force that knew I simply needed to have some fun again. We really were great together, and each of us satisfied the other's need for light-hearted companionship, and good, old-fashioned moral support.

School was getting more difficult, as we were now beginning to see patients. As well, we were going through the hardest part of the battle to become doctors – the National Board Exams: four very difficult theoretical and practical exams that could make or break a person's dreams to practice chiropractic. While Dave and I *did* study, we also invoked the power of positive thinking. When all of our friends were pouring over the textbooks on the night before each big exam, Dave and I made it a rule to leave the books behind and have a good time. We saw U2, my all-time favourite band, before one board exam, and we went dancing with the "Super Freak", Rick James, before another. The point was that we were too tired the next day to get stressed about failing the exam, and always ended up doing relatively well. It really ticked our fellow classmates off, but we got near enough to the same results without killing ourselves with stress in the process.

The old Doctor joke was true.

"What do you call a student that scores very high on the board exams?"

"Doctor."

"And what do you call a student that gets an average score on the board exams?"

"Doctor."

I don't know about you, but I would prefer to attend a doctor that knows a little bit about life, because she lived it, rather than memorised it out of a textbook.

A Shock at Homecoming

One of the highlights of the year was a celebration at school called Lyceum. This was a tradition that B.J. Palmer, developer of chiropractic, and son of its founder, D.D. Palmer, had originated at Palmer Chiropractic College, many years earlier. It was a time for alumni to reunite, for students to host and entertain, for philosophical debates, personal testimonies, music and lectures from great international speakers. I had the privilege of meeting Dan Millman, author of *Way of the Peaceful Warrior*, the very first spiritual novel I had read. As President of the Student Body, I was honoured when asked to do the introduction for Marlo Morgan, author of *Mutant Message Down Under*. I was inspired by her adventurous spirit and so impressed by her very clear message of the need this world has to get its act together, fast. We had the opportunity to mingle with some very influential doctors from the international circuit, and the highlight of the weekend was always the dinner banquet and dance.

Dave had decided not to stay around for Lyceum, because it was May, the busy season for landscaping. It was a shame, because I had an awesome dress, and the theme of the night was old New Orleans and jazz. I missed having him there, because he was so much fun, and I loved the way he danced! I managed to have a great time anyway with all of my friends, and even had an encounter with the spirit world, quite unexpectedly.

When Ben and I had lived in Charleston, the food we ate most on our limited budget was shrimp. His family would cast for shrimp every season and then freeze them to eat throughout the year. In the foothills of Virginia, shrimp was a very expensive delicacy, so I was in heaven, eating it nearly every second day, for free! What I didn't know was that in those couple of years, I had eaten a lifetime quota of shellfish. It's much like getting stung by bees at different stages in your life, with no reaction at all. Then one day, a bee stings you, and you nearly die.

On the night of the banquet, my body decided that in terms of shellfish consumption, enough was enough. Because the theme was New Orleans, the main dish was crayfish, a much larger and uglier version of the shrimp. I sat down at the table and began to dig in, when all of a sudden my head began to spin. My lips started to tingle, and at first, my throat felt numb, then it started to swell shut. I ran in to the bathroom and got sick several times. Even after throwing up, it still felt as if I was breathing through a drinking straw, and I was really getting scared because I knew I was going into anaphylactic shock.

One of the doctors staying in the hotel where the banquet was held offered for my friends to take me up to his room while they rang for the ambulance. I remember lying on the floor, my eyes rolling back into my head and I could feel *I really did not want to go!* Suddenly, I could hear a very familiar sound in the background as people were talking to me and to each other.

The buzz that came before the whoosh, that had carried me to the heavens twice before, was getting closer. This time, my head rolled to one side, and who did I see hovering in the corner? There were two very familiar apparitions; the guides that had accompanied me on this memorable journey before.

191

They seemed to be smiling, but oddly enough, it didn't feel like they were preparing to take me anywhere. It was as if they were only watching, overseeing the situation with their reassuring presence. The next thing I felt was a hand on my face, turning my head away from my spiritual spectators.

"Look at me, *do not* look at them. It's not time," a voice said.

Donald Epstein, an amazing chiropractor and the founder of Network Spinal Analysis, was kneeling down beside me. He made a few gentle impulses to strategic points on my body, and almost immediately, as if by magic, I could feel the swelling going down in my throat. I knew that I was now out of danger and was going to be fine. I was so fortunate that he had been there, and even luckier that his son had been my own chiropractor, and a close friend. He had run to get his father when he realised I was in serious trouble. After all of the drama had passed, and I was feeling better, I simply *had* to ask Dr. Epstein,

"You could see the men in the corner of the room, couldn't you?"

He acknowledged he had, and then went on to share some very beautiful anecdotes from his own life. His stories reassured me that I was not in this alone, and his remarkable skill and kind reassurance made such an impact on me. Once again, I had faced a porthole of exit, an opportunity to check out of this world, and I definitively knew . . . *it just wasn't time.*

Sink or Swim

Dave and I spent a lot of our free time basking in the fabulous South Carolina sunshine even though I had given up sunbathing a few years earlier, in an attempt to save myself a few wrinkles. Dave was a bronzed God. He loved to stretch out out in the sun, and because I loved spending time with him, I started to tan my skin again, every spare moment I could get. Many were the days that I went to see patients covered in oil, with a bikini on underneath my clinic jacket. Whenever we could, we would hop in his truck and drive the three and a half hours to Charleston to soak up the sun on the beach.

Skipping school one day, we took a day trip and sprawled out on the beach: Dave with his earphones and music on; I, dozing in and out of consciousness in the glorious heat under a bright blue sky.

"HELP, HELP!" broke my sun-filled daze.

I sat up and took a good look around. Nobody seemed to be rushing, or responding, to cries for help. I looked out to the sea, and at the end of a concrete jetty, I could see a child bobbing up and down in the waves, clearly struggling to stay above water. I thought it strange that no one else seemed to hear, or see her, because I could hear her as if she were right next to me. I went running into the water and swam out to the girl. She was being bashed by the incoming tide. I wrapped my arms around her, only to discover that she wasn't budging. She had somehow gotten her foot wedged into the rocks at the base of the jetty. I knew I would shred her foot if I pulled it out, but it certainly beat the alternative. I gave a good hard yank and tore her foot away from the sharp stones.

As anyone who has ever been a lifeguard knows, at this point, you are nearly in more danger than the victim, as their panic sets in, and the sinking swimmer grabs on to you for dear life. She was no more than ten, and I was a robust twenty-seven years old, but at that moment, the tables turned, and I found myself submerged, struggling to get to the surface again. In an eerie moment of calm, I remember saying to myself,

"Oh no, I'm going to drown *again*!"

I spent several seconds in this oddly tranquil space, and then I gathered my senses, sprung to the top, grabbed her around the waist, and dragged her back to the shore.

People were now gathering as they realised that something was amiss. Her parents rushed over – they hadn't even noticed her gone – and Dave had just discovered that I was no longer by his side. The little girl was fine, bar needing a few stitches in her foot. I was on an adrenaline rush that lasted for the rest of the day. I find it very interesting that I love the water and have absolutely no fear of it, or of drowning, only memories of having been there before, but under very different circumstances. The theme of drowning had seemed to follow me since childhood, always reminding me that this wasn't my first time on this planet.

One Point for Psychic Suzy

I had met some people from a college in Bournemouth, England, during an international conference for chiropractic students earlier in the year. As President of the student body, I was invited to go to Bournemouth to visit the school and to speak to the students about the philosophy on which Sherman College had been built. I had never been overseas before, and I had to come up with a crafty way to get the school to fund the trip.

Dr. Koch, my former teacher, and always my friend, was now the President of the college. I went to him to plead my case, and he lovingly laughed at my desperate attempt to convince him of why my trip to England was essential to the growth and forward advancement of the college. I felt like I was thirteen again, trying every trick in the book to persuade my parents to let me go to my first concert, Chicago (I was very convincing that the band Chicago was calm and decent, and it wasn't going to be a wild rock gig). My parents will attest to the fact that my negotiating skills were a force to be reckoned with, so Chicago *was*, in fact, my first live band, and fourteen years later, *I was going abroad*! It seemed that Psychic Suzy was right, after all.

Chapter 22

Ode to Ireland

We are the music – makers,

And we are the dreamers of dreams,

Wandering by lone sea – breakers,

And sitting by desolate streams:

World – losers and world – forsakers,

On whom the pale moon gleams;

Yet we are the movers and shakers

Of the world for ever, it seems.

We, in the ages lying,

In the buried past of the earth,

Built Ninevah with our sighing,

And Babel itself with our mirth:

And o'erthrew them with prophesying

To the old of the new world's worth;

For each age is a dream that is dying,

Or one that is coming to birth.

- Arthur O' Shaughnessy

On a Wing and a Prayer

At this point in my life, I hadn't flown too many times (at least not in an airplane!). I wasn't afraid of dying, but the thoughts of going down in a plane, and dying with a bunch of *other people*, really unnerved me. I had always seen my death as a sort of "one woman show". I had taken a flight to Florida once on a small plane that had the propellers on the wings. Towards the end of the trip, one of the propellers began to slow down, and then stop, and the plane took a dip to one side. I was squashed into the seat next to a very large, very nervous, and very sweaty Southern belle.

"Oh my God!" she yelled out. "We're going down!"

The flight attendant immediately rushed down the aisle to keep her from panicking the other passengers, assuring her, that we could make it just fine on one engine. She squirmed, fidgeted, whimpered, and moaned the rest of the way, and quite frankly, *I've never been right since*! One of the pitfalls of being so sensitive to energies and people's feelings is that when I find myself in confined spaces with a lot of people, I really feel anxious. Their excitement and their fears seem to stick to me like a magnet, and I feel as if I am being taken over by emotions that don't even belong to me. Mediation and concentration have helped over the years, but my first overseas flight was tough, and I had "white knuckles" all the way from New York to London.

My only distraction was my friend Lee, a girl from Spartanburg, who was travelling with me en route to Amsterdam. I was introduced to her by my housemate Jo, and when she heard that I was heading to the British Isles, she asked if she could tag along. I welcomed her constant chatter, as it kept me from ripping the arms off of my seat on the flight over!

Green In More Ways than One

The doctor that had invited me to come to the U.K. was originally from Dublin. We met him in London first and then flew over to Ireland for a week, before I headed back to England to visit the school, and Lee took off for Amsterdam.

Fifty-seven viewings of classic film, *The Quiet Man*, had prepared me for stone walls, rolling green fields, and lots and lots of sheep. I was very surprised then, when I arrived into the cosmopolitan

196

city of Dublin, with its fantastic character, and a buzz comparable to that of any major city I had ever been to.

Our host's sister was kind enough to loan her car to us, so we could go explore the country on our own. The Doc had business to attend to, and would meet up with us when we returned to Dublin. We were amazed by all of the beautiful little villages, and the fact that there seemed to be a pub on every corner. We stopped about an hour and a half outside of Dublin, in the midlands town of Athlone, because we saw a sign for a Chiropractor and I wanted to stop in and see what an Irish practice was like.

We were greeted by a very friendly receptionist named Maureen. We clicked immediately and she had a twinkle in her eye that I loved straight away. She introduced us to the doctor, a guy originally from Canada. I liked the feel of the office and began to visualise what it would be like if it were mine. The Canadian doctor spoke of how difficult he found it to live in Ireland because it lacked many of the "creature comforts" of home. I thought to myself, that it should be me, not him, running that office. At that moment, I had the funniest feeling, that one day *I would be*.

We expressed our thanks and said our goodbyes, then walked into town and across the river Shannon to the most beautiful cathedral. Across the road was a *real* castle, something the average American doesn't see every day. It was perched on the bank of the river, like an ancient guardian of history, and down the hill, just behind it, was Sean's Bar, Ireland's oldest pub. We laughed, because in our few short days in Ireland, we had been told about ten different pubs that were meant to be the oldest in the country, but when we walked in, it was like stepping back in time, with sawdust on the floors, and low ceilings covered in paraphernalia from all around the world. This turned out to be the real McCoy, Sean's Bar did, in fact, proudly hold the record as Ireland's oldest public house. There were musicians playing that night, so we decided we would stay and check it out. By the next morning, I was in love with this town. During our travels, people would laugh at me when I said that my favourite place had been Athlone.

"There are so many beautiful places along the coast and in the majestic hills, why an old garrison town like Athlone?"

There was magic, and music in the air of that old town, and something about it had captured my heart, forever. If ever I had been somewhere that I felt I had been before, I loved this place as if I was the prodigal child returning home, at last.

We woke the next morning, not too bright and early, because the session from the night before had gone into the wee hours of the morning. My ears were still ringing with the sounds of guitars, pipes and the bodhran (the native Irish drum). Real Irish music, in a real Irish pub, played by people that looked as if they were having the time of their lives; this was a sight that I had never seen in any bar at home. The people were there to enjoy each other, and to share their talent, and I felt so at home in that environment.

Being "fresh off the boat" from America, I was unaccustomed to the *colourful* Irish slang that I was introduced to that night. The "F" word featured at least twice in every sentence, by young and old, alike. Even those that looked like the sweet, little, Granny types, used the word to describe everything from the f***ing horrible weather, to the f***ing brilliant day they had with the grandkids! I nearly fainted when I was asked if I had enjoyed the crack! That was a nasty illegal drug sold in the back alleys in America; in Ireland, the *craic* means "a great time had by all." I really found it funny that a girl from the South was constantly being referred to as a "Yank." Where I come from, a "Yank" is someone who lives up North, like in New York or Boston, and is a name you don't call a self-respecting, citizen of the South! Obviously, they had never seen *Gone with the Wind*!

The Right Direction on the Wrong Side of the Road

We hit the road, heading West for Galway, clueless to the fact that things were about to get *very interesting*. We got to Eyre Square, in the centre of Galway, and wandered through the side streets, meandering through all of the quaint little shops. We went into an antique jewellery store and had a nose around. My stomach began to turn flips when I picked up a necklace with a marking that was now very familiar. It was etched with one of the twenty-one symbols that had haunted me for the last three months. Breathless, I took the necklace to the shopkeeper and asked if he knew anything about the symbol. He said that it was a character from an ancient Celtic script, which was found thousands of years ago in Ireland. I was so thrilled as I called Lee over to have a look. I had filled her in about the symbols on the flight over, and I couldn't believe I was now holding a replica of one in my hands.

I was starting to get that feeling; the sense that something incredible was about to unfold. We walked across the square and into a pub called Fibber McGee's. We were making ourselves at home, sitting at a table, talking to an Irish couple; when a friend of theirs sat down to join us. His name was Brian, and he was fantastic, with his red hair and freckles: "Ginger'" as the Irish called it. He was a good-looking fellow, and really friendly as well, and when his friends told him that we were touring around the country, he offered to show us a few of the sights. We were grateful to be shown around by someone who knew where he was going, and by someone who knew how to drive on the left side of the road. We had been lucky to make it as far as we had without completely destroying the passenger side of our friend's car.

Brian met us the next morning, and we drove through the rocky landscape of the Burren, and then the rolling, green hillsides of

Connemarra. Two days later, we arrived in the evening to the town of Lisdoonvarna, famous for its matchmaking festival for eager young bucks and beautiful Irish lasses. We stopped to have a bite to eat in a classic old pub and while Lee and I finished up, Brian disappeared for a few minutes. When he returned, he pulled me aside, and said that he wanted to give me something to say thanks for bringing him along. He handed me a silver ring, with a twisted, Celtic design. I was delighted and told him how much we appreciated him taking the time to show two complete strangers around his homeland. I put the ring on my finger, and that's when I noticed it. Inscribed in a tiny marking, within the design, *was another one of the symbols*.

"Where did you get this?" I quizzed him.

"Just over there, in the shop; if you don't like it . . ."

"No, no! I love it! But I need to see where you got this!"

He took me across the road and showed me a tray of rings that all were of similar design. There must have been over thirty of them, and I frantically started looking through each and every one to see if they were all the same. Brian was looking at me like I was some sort of lunatic, but at the time, he knew nothing about the symbols, *or the girl that was chasing them*. Of all of the rings, the one that he had picked for me was the only one in the tray that was marked with one of the twenty- one symbols.

After my strange behaviour, Brian demanded to know what was going on. We sat down, and I told him a condensed version of my life story that ended with flaming symbols which now appeared to be of Irish origins. He grinned from ear to ear, taking me by the hand, saying, "Get in the car; I know where we're heading next."

Midnight Sun

It was already late, but Ireland in the summer was much different than home. The night time sky didn't get dark until almost midnight, and the sunset seemed to last for hours. Brian drove like mad, heading East, but would not tell us where we were going. Eventually, as we approached our destination, I felt the hair stand up on the back of my neck. The sensation that something incredible was about to happen had never left since we had arrived in Galway. But now, it had escalated to a sense that I was about to uncover a great secret, the essence of my true self; something my spiritual guides had insured me would happen, in the not so distant future. We pulled up to Newgrange, a megalithic passage tomb in the Boyne Valley, built some five thousand years earlier. The historical monument had closed hours earlier, as it was now after ten-thirty. I didn't care, though, because there, on the entrance gates were replicas of the symbols inside, cast in wrought iron. I couldn't believe what I was seeing, even if it was only the padlocked gates leading into the grounds.

Brian said that there were kerbstones all around the tomb, covered in symbols that had been found to predate the Celts by 2500 years. This was my light switch; a connection so powerful that I knew in an instant I had found my way home. I didn't even need to see the quartz-covered burial mound to know that this was the beacon that had so boldly sent its signal to guide me to the next phase of my journey. I stood in tears, so totally united with my surroundings that I got a fright when Brian grabbed me, saying,

"Come on, your leaving tomorrow, you may never get this chance again!"

Before I knew what was happening, we were running across a field, trespassing on a farmer's private property, so that we could hop the fence and get a look at the tomb, close up. I wasn't intending to break the law that night, but when I touched the stones, so deeply carved by ancient hands, I just lived for the moment; it was only a moment, though, as I was snapped back to reality by the sound of barking dogs and the lights of an approaching vehicle. We ran through the fields and emerged the other side, covered in cow poop and God knows what else! The evening light was fading into the royal blue of midnight, and the three of us laughed excitedly, celebrating as if we had just discovered the Holy Grail.

Removing the Blinders

The following day, Lee and I said our goodbyes and promised to catch up when we were back in the States. I flew to England, where I was to encounter an entirely different way of life than I had just experienced in Ireland. I had felt so at home there, and my time had been spent just getting to know the people and the places and had ended with the momentous occasion of finding the ancient symbols. England was an entirely different kettle of fish. A melting pot of diverse cultures, I quickly realised what a sheltered life I had led. My lack of knowledge about the rest of the world was not only was embarrassing, but also made me feel a little on the dumb side. The people that I encountered were so different than any others I had ever met, and the lifestyle was completely new to me. Everything in London seemed so crowded and stuck together. The houses were terraced, the cars were tiny, and nothing was "all you can eat" I hadn't seemed to notice these things in Ireland, because my focus had been on something entirely different, all together.

Thinking of home, it seemed so strange now, and I began to understand the worldwide perception of America as being a gluttonous society. Our cars were big, our houses were big, our food consumption was big, and our knowledge of the way the rest of the world lives, now seemed very, very small. Don't get me wrong. I loved my home, and its people, but my eyes were opening to the possibility that the land of the free and the home of the brave was sorely lacking in a few crucial areas, at least in my neck of the woods. I was challenged by complete strangers, about my views on America's involvement in world politics and its contribution to the consumption and energy crisis. I was asked for my opinion on Third World debt and how I felt about the formation of a European Union. For a girl that had been well-educated in the American school systems, through a university and now about to become a doctor, I suddenly realised I knew very little about the rest of the world, and I knew for certain, *I wasn't alone*.

I had a lot to learn, and I would make it my business to remove my blinders, to become a citizen of the world, not just my own country. The mess this planet is in was now making a whole lot of sense to me, and my personal ignorance to the ways of the rest of the world was not a good enough excuse. If nothing else had happened, this realisation would have made the whole trip worthwhile.

International Flavour

The difference between the energy in England and Ireland was palpable. Ireland seemed so relaxed and easy going, while England felt much faster paced and hectic. I hadn't made it out of London yet, so when I headed down country, I began to see what made the English countryside so famous. I felt like I was travelling back through time, minus the super highways that made getting from A to B a whole lot easier than travelling the potholed roads of Ireland. The land was majestic, and the pace of life began to slow down the closer we got to the shore.

The chiropractic college in Bournemouth was outstanding. It was located in a quaint seaside town that reeked of history. The grounds were beautiful, and I couldn't believe my eyes when I was given a tour of the school that ended in the college bar! They had a bar right there in the school! Dorothy was no longer in Kansas, and Toto was in the school bar having a pint of lager! I'd never witnessed anything like it! Where I come from, there's a church on every corner. In this lovely town, and in most others I had seen, there were churches *and* pubs, everywhere you turned.

The students were friendly and hailed from all over the globe. I had never really had the opportunity to mingle with so many people, from so many different places, all at the same time. I found myself gravitating towards the Irish students, because I seemed to feel more at home with the way they spoke, and their fantastic sense of humour. I also had a lot to talk about, having just returned from Ireland a few days earlier. Everyone was very nice, but they all got a big kick out of the fact that I had short hair and wore overalls, or dungarees, as they called them. I explained that they were very fashionable at home, and they were quick to point out that I wasn't in the South anymore! They said I had better not expect any men to approach me, because in England, a *straight* girl did not, under any circumstances, dress like that!

I hate to say it, but they were right. I didn't heed the advice, and when I was taken to a nightclub, the only people that even looked at me, much less spoke to me, were the ones I had come with. The fashion was so dramatically different than what I was accustomed to. The girls were dressed to the nines just to go out for a few drinks, and everyone looked as if they had just walked out of the hairdressers. It was very impressive, but one thing that really shocked me was how the girls were wearing tiny little skirts, sleeveless tops and very high heels with no stockings in the bitter English air. No one seemed to mind the cold, and no one was willing to cover up a fabulous outfit for the sake of a bit of warmth.

My new friends found me comical. I had a heavy twang when I spoke, and I dressed even funnier than I talked, and when I danced . . . oh, the laughs of them all. The techno beat of European dance music was a far cry from Lynyrd Skynyrd or Guns 'N' Roses. I think they enjoyed having me around, though, because they felt as if I fit every American stereotype known to man. I was nearly too humorous to be true. Regardless of their motives, the students were all very welcoming, and included me in all of their activities, both in school, and out.

I went to a house party hosted by some of the students where I met a girl called Maryellen, and we became fast friends, for life. She introduced me around, and on that same night, I met a man that was to become a major feature in my life the following year, and for all the years to follow. John was from Ireland and had a personality the size of Texas. It was friendship at first sight, and I think both of us would agree that we knew that we had known one another before. Remember, soul mates come in many forms, and one of mine had just appeared with a pint of Guinness and a head full of "Southern Rock." John had lived in America and travelled it extensively, and he was as knowledgeable about my country, *and* my favourite bands, as any good southern-fried soul. He shook his head in disbelief, as I told him about sneaking into the burial tomb at Newgrange, but seemed to totally understand the reasons behind my actions and couldn't wait to hear more. I think he recognised my genuine awe and respect for his country, and being one that followed his intuition as well, he appreciated the mission that I was on. I didn't get to spend a lot of time with John on that trip, but knew in my heart, that the fun with him had only just begun.

I made a few talks to several of the classes at the college, and my gratitude and appreciation for the chance to be educated with Sherman's solid philosophical foundation was immense. These students knew the anatomy of the body and the scientific approach to chiropractic, but most were completely lacking in its philosophy. If we had been taught one thing at Sherman, it was that chiropractic was a science, an art *and* a philosophy; each as important as the other. These students had been told stories of the strange practitioners in America that saw chiropractic as a religion and prayed to the God of innate intelligence. After hearing the truth, many of the future doctors found themselves wanting to know more. Some just laughed and rubbished the idea that owning a personal philosophy would make any difference to running a successful practice.

Unfortunately, chiropractic would just become a job to those people, until they grasped the fundamentals of owning its philosophy. It takes all three sides to complete the triad, and thank goodness, there were some very motivated students, particularly my friends John and Maryellen, that were interested in stepping outside of the box. I had done my fair share of public speaking at Sherman, but when I got the opportunity to stand in front of new faces, with new ideas, I knew that somewhere down the line, I would love to teach. I loved the challenge of being challenged, because when it came to chiropractic philosophy, I knew my stuff.

My Irish host in England was like no one I have ever met. He had the tenacity of a Bulldog when it came to taking on the system, with a confidence and attitude that would see him become one of the greats in this field. After we spent a couple of days at the school, he took me to see a few of the sights around London, and I was particularly excited when he suggested that we go to Stonehenge. I wasn't sure what to think, as I had fallen prey to my own imagination of what I thought this place that had baffled the world for so many years would look like. It was much smaller than I had pictured it to be, and it was also roped off so that you couldn't actually walk through it. After my experience at Newgrange in Ireland, it didn't really stand a chance. The *layout* of the stones, however, sparked a memory, more like a familiar feeling, the details of which I had forgotten. There was a magic surrounding this mysterious site, and I was grateful for the opportunity to be there.

My trip came to an end, all too soon, and I hated the thoughts of returning to the grind of classes and exams. I left my new friends, vowing to see them again, very soon, even though I knew that the likelihood of a return trip any time in the near future was basically nonexistent. I had two more terms of school to complete and would spend the next year sitting State and National Board Exams. Still, I hoped that I would find my way back, because now I was hooked, and I could easily see myself returning to this part of the world, to live.

If it's Meant to Be…

In the last quarter of school, students were given the chance to do an externship (work experience) in the practice of a doctor who was sanctioned by the school board. If a student opted not to do this, the last term was spent continuing to practice in the school's health centre. I introduced the idea of externing abroad to the school board, and found out that several of the school's alumni were practicing in Ireland. I worked hard to come up with contacts, and ultimately was to become the first student to do an international externship. I had never met the doctor that I would be working with, but my friend Maryellen in England knew someone that knew someone, and it all came together.

When I made the decision, I ran it past Dave, and we decided, that because I would be leaving at Christmas, that we would stop seeing each other for the remaining months before I left. I guess we all love a little drama in our lives. That idea lasted a whole week, before we realised how stupid it was! We made up our minds to have the time of our lives, and when it was time to say goodbye, we'd leave it at that. Those next few months were amazing and probably some of the best times I have ever had. Those memories are precious to me, and we lived every moment *in* the moment.

Christmas break of 1997 came like a tidal wave. I had to pack up my home of the last four years, leave the security of college life and its friends, bid farewell to an amazing man, and see my family before heading to England, and ultimately Ireland. My flight was to leave on Christmas Eve, and I would arrive bright and early on Christmas Day in London. On the day before I was to fly out, we got the news that Grandmother Clark had passed away. The very first thing that my Aunt Joyce said to me was that I had made a promise to Grandmother a year earlier. I was supposed to sing at my grandmother's funeral whenever she died, but I had also given her my word that I would not allow singing at her funeral to interfere with school commitments. I had forgotten this promise, probably because I had *no intention* of keeping it in the first place. Of course, I would delay the trip and stay for the funeral. Even in her failing health, Grandmother was well aware that I was to make the trip abroad. She had been so excited for me to have this opportunity; it was *her* parents that were from England and Wales and her grandparents that were from Northern Ireland. For me to make this journey meant the world to her, the chance to visit my roots, to follow my destiny, and I was now faced with a serious dilemma. I wanted to be there for my mother, but my mother insisted that I take the trip, without delay. I ended up going to the church and recording the song that was played at her funeral. I made the flight to the U.K. the following day. I was never sure about the decision, but in the end, I did what she asked me to do, and had to be content with my choice.

Chapter 23

You may never know what results come from your action. But if you do nothing, there will be
No results. - **Mahatma Gandhi**

A Change of Plans

I arrived in London on Christmas morning, feeling a little worse for the wear from the all night flight, and due to the fact that I was missing my Grandmother's funeral. My fog lifted the second I saw my friend, Maryellen, waiting for me in arrivals. She was so happy to see me, and was to be my hostess for the next two weeks, while I awaited instructions from the doctor that I would be working with in Ireland. We quickly caught up on events from the last six months on the drive back to Bournemouth. Maryellen was a couple of years behind me in school, but had a real grasp of the fundamentals of chiropractic, and its philosophy. She couldn't wait to hear all of my news about board exams, the last two terms of school, and how I had left things with my boyfriend, Dave. We looked like two old hens, clucking down the road, in her little purple banger of a car, affectionately known as "Barney."

The next week was wonderful, as we spent time looking around the countryside and developing our friendship. None of the other students were around, since most had gone home for the holidays. Maryellen was on a student's budget and going home to Canada for Christmas had not been a realistic prospect for her that year. We had a great time, topped off by a quick trip to Ireland for New Year's Eve. I thought I had died and gone to heaven (pun intended)! I met up again with my friend John, from Ireland. We had met in England the summer before, and I now loved watching him in action on his home turf. What a character and what an introduction to the Irish way of life! The weekend trip ended much too soon, and we headed back to Bournemouth, to wait for word from the doctor I would be working with in Dublin.

Things weren't going exactly as planned, and I was having difficulty getting in touch with my new boss in Ireland. I spent a lot longer in England than I was supposed to, but as with all things, I trusted that there must be a purpose behind it all. The time was well spent, living it up, unwinding after the last five years of study. I also cultivated my relationship with John, enjoying every second spent his company. I was mesmerised with his wit, wisdom and amazing approach to life. I adored John, because he was the kind of guy that would see a girl walk by, maybe a little overweight, *not* Barbie doll attractive, and he would pick her greatest feature then comment on how fabulous she was! His ability to see the beauty in everyone was incredible. I had come from a culture that was way too hung up on a perfect body image; unfortunately sending out the wrong message about what real beauty was all about.

When the time came for my long-awaited stay in Ireland, things weren't exactly the way they were supposed to be. The doctor I was working for had some unforeseen issues arise, and it meant that I would have to spend some of my time elsewhere. I was excited at the prospect of getting to see, and work, in more than one area, so it suited me just fine! He was a lovely, gentle sort of man, and I learned more than just Chiropractic while in his company. He taught me a thing or two about attitude, outlook, and maturity, as well.

With a stroke of luck, I was taken under the wing of what I still consider to be one of the most extraordinary individuals I have ever met. Dr. D was larger than life, lived to the max, knew the most amazing people and had travelled to places that I had never even heard of. He had graduated from chiropractic school over fifteen years ago and had returned to Ireland to practice, enjoying success at a very young age. He immediately put me to work in a clinic that he owned in Limerick. I was a little nervous at first, but I can honestly say, that to this day, I loved the people of there, and found it to be one of the most exciting, and wonderful places I have ever lived.

There were two American doctors, both whom had recently relocated to Ireland, working to build the new practice. I moved in with them, and in between nights on the town, sight-seeing, and a lot of laughter, I helped them in any way that I could in the practice. They were well used to the Irish lifestyle, and one day when they sent me to buy some office supplies, I realised that I was not yet so used to it!

I was dressed in a min-skirt and high boots (I had long since ditched the dungarees) and was walking out of the shop with my arms full of supplies. Two policemen (or gardai as they are called in Ireland) were walking towards me. I must have had the look of confusion that only a blonde can get, when they asked me if I was alright. In my thick Southern accent and my short skirt and long boots I replied,

" No thanks, I'm just waiting for a ride."

Well they buckled in two, unable to contain their laughter and explained to me that in Ireland, a ride meant shag.

"Shag, you mean like the dance?" (The Shag is South Carolina's state dance).

Now one of them had now been brought to tears from laughter as he again tried to explain a ride and shag. Finally, I turned bright red as I realised that I was standing on a street corner dressed like something out of *Pretty Woman* and had just told them that I was waiting for sex! From that day forward I made it my business to learn all of the Irish slang I could.

The experience was unforgettable, and the friendships, I treasured. What had appeared to be a possible hiccup in my training was turning out to be the most valuable practical experience I could have asked for.

When my time in Ireland came to an end, I had a meeting with Dr. D, in a place called the K Club just outside of Dublin. I had never heard of it before, but most of the world has now heard of it, as it hosted the world famous Ryder cup golf tournament in 2007. It was an incredible facility, stunningly beautiful and host to many famous faces. I went to the toilet shortly after we had arrived and walked past a member of the famous Spice Girl band in the hallway. I didn't stay star struck for long though, because I was there to try and negotiate my future in Ireland. We went into a private room, and as Dr. D sipped champagne, I told him that I would do whatever it took to return to his country to live. He was very sympathetic to my plea, but the reality was, that even with all of the offices he owned, there were no positions available. It wasn't as simple as hopping on a plane and setting up shop. There were visas, and sponsorships that had to be obtained, then there was the little matter of three hundred and fifty thousand pounds, (if you wanted to set up on your own) without getting hired under a working visa. I was three hundred and forty-nine thousand short, so that wasn't an option. Distraught, but determined, I packed my bags and headed home, only two days before another big landmark in my life – graduating from student to doctor.

The Lawn Doctor

Dave picked me up from the airport, and he laughed when he saw my additional baggage. Not the suitcases, but the fifteen extra pounds I had packed on while overseas! Graduation was an amazing time, and I was so glad to be spending it with Dave. I really had missed him, but could see that our lives were beginning to separate and move in different directions.

Dave and I had a frank discussion about what we were going to do. As pragmatic as ever, Dave said that he knew that my ultimate goal was to go and work with "the leprechauns". But wouldn't it make much more sense to stay for the year, complete my final board exam the following November, and then look into moving over? He suggested that I move up to Philadelphia; help him for the summer with the landscaping business while preparing to sit the most difficult of the board exams. We had also both wanted to take the South Carolina exam, for nostalgia's sake, as well as for the experience. I said that it sounded like a good plan and prepared myself to become a Yankee!

That summer, the fifteen pounds that I had gained in Ireland melted off during the fourteen hour work days that Dave and I were putting in. It was in the upper nineties every day, and let me tell you, pushing a lawn mower around gigantic apartment complexes was anything but glamorous. I remember being covered in sweat, muck and smelling like a wild animal when this beautiful, little thing swished her way across the freshly cut grass at one of the complexes. She was dressed like a Barbie and looked like one too. She marched right up to Dave, who of course, was glistening with sweat, muscles bulging, looking like Mr. July in some pin-up calendar. She was an ex-girlfriend that "just happened" to wiggle by to say hello. I didn't even bother getting upset, because with the way I looked and smelled . . . it just didn't matter! Anyway, I didn't want to appear jealous or too concerned, because I knew that my future laid waiting in Ireland. Even though Dave and I had an understanding, I didn't want either of us to become too comfortable or attached to my temporary status as an outdoor labourer, a resident of Philadelphia, or as a girlfriend.

Fractured Dreams

Money was really tight that year. We were working hard, but between trying to set up a place to practice, and paying for the exams

213

we were taking (and re-taking in my case), we were broke. I can still remember the day that Dave said I was going to have to find a way to contribute more to the fledgling practice than the wages he was paying me. With great reluctance, I took the wedding ring that I had invested so much time and energy into, seven years earlier, and handed it over to what can only be described as a jewellery shark. I sold the ring for so much less than it was worth, but I was under a lot of pressure, and honestly, it was time to let it go. We purchased our first chiropractic table for adjusting the spine, and temporarily, this contribution was enough.

Behind the scenes, I was constantly researching ways to get back to Ireland. It had gone from mission to obsession. I was in touch with my friends on the Emerald Isle, hoping that something would give. Nothing was turning up, and my enthusiasm was turning to frustration.

The time came for Dave and me to sit the South Carolina Board Exam. It was really fun, heading back to our alma mater, and we enjoyed reconnecting with some of our old friends and our favourite haunts. The exam was going smoothly, until I got into a room with a couple of doctors that were going to ask me to diagnose some hideous neurological disorder. True to form, my subconscious ability to summon injury, or illness, during times of stress reared its ugly, little head. I was struggling to come up with the appropriate words, when one of the doctors went to move a very heavy, wooden chair. The chair toppled over, directly hitting the top of my foot. We could nearly hear each of the THREE fractures, as my bones cracked under the weight of the chair. Needless to say, not only did I give a "very explicit" answer to their question, but I was whizzed through the rest of the exam.

Getting Legless

During that summer, I had the opportunity to work with a legendary chiropractic couple, Drs. Reggie and Irene Gold. For him, I helped out with a couple of projects he was working on regarding chiropractic philosophy, but it was his wife that really put me to work! She was the leading authority and Queen of the National Board Exam Reviews. Hers was a service that most students availed of, taking them through rigorous preparation courses for the exams. I think I actually learned more in the short time that I taught for her, than I did my entire time in school. The information was condensed, taught with rhymes, songs, pictures and endless repetition. Her system was incredible, and highly successful, and she was a genius at her work. I enjoyed the time I spent travelling and teaching, further convincing me that eventually, I would wind up some sort of a teacher. She knew a little about my curious history and would laugh every time we went through a security check in the airport. I would have to be searched, because my *unusual* energetic constitution never failed to set the alarms off.

One of her requirements was that I sit as many boards as I could, to further increase my knowledge of what her customers could expect. What a nightmare! In essence, I had spent the last twenty-four years of my life in school, and now I was willingly subjecting myself to one exam after another in order to become a more proficient teacher. Dave thought I was nuts. Most days, so did I. It wasn't until I went to sit in on the prep course for the New York State Board that it all became worth it.

I was still in a ridiculous looking plaster cast and "shoe" because of my broken foot. I entered the meeting room of the hotel, where the review was being held, late as usual. I sauntered in, walking as if I had arrived on horseback rather than by car. The awkward plaster boot was very difficult to walk with, and everyone looked sympathetically at me; everyone but one.

This guy was big, I mean body builder big, and made no attempt to hide the fact that he was amused at the way I was walking. In fact, he even commented,

"Cute girl, shame about the affliction!"

If he hadn't been so hot, I would've decked him! I sat and listened, as best I could with this bear of a man constantly making smart comments under his breath, which I must admit, were pretty funny. When class finally ended, I was prepared to take him to task, when he stood up, and began to walk out of the room . . . like an ape!

I thought he was making fun of me at first, until I noticed that his pant leg was hung on something silver; his titanium prosthetic. This guy was missing a leg. Now I felt bad and I couldn't say anything, *until I got to know Mike.* Within five minutes of meeting up with Mike and the others in the hotel bar, I realised that not only did he have one prosthetic, but there were two! Along with his fake legs; he had lost them when hit by a drunk and drugged up driver; he had the most incredible outlook and an even better sense of humour! He was married to the physiotherapist that had nursed him through his post-accident rehabilitation, and they had *seven* fabulous kids. He was a success as a chiropractor, and a competitive athlete. As far as he was concerned, who needed legs?

Out of respect to his wife (I mean this in the most honourable way), if he had not been married, I would have run off with him that very day! We were kindred spirits and to this day remain the best of friends. Getting to know Mike was a great fringe benefit of having to sit, yet another, board exam.

Mike and his family lived in New Jersey, just across the bridge from where Dave and I were located. Dave really liked Mike as well, and he was perfectly content to send me off to take the exam with him. On the big day, Mike and I made our way to the test facility, somewhere in New York. I was still in plaster, and Mike was on his legs, not in his wheel chair. We looked like a pair of drunks, staggering into the exam on our wobbly limbs.

We were in a big room, watching the other students cram last minute information into their already saturated brains. Of course, Mike and I were messing around, refusing to stress out. The exam administrator came up to me, having seen my plastered foot, and asked if I would require any assistance during the exam. His concern was about time, as the exam stations only allowed three minutes each, and he was afraid that I would waste time getting from station to station. He obviously had not seen Mike walk in.

I told him that I thought I would be fine, but before I could finish my sentence, I heard Mike's thick Jersey accent interject,

"Yo, dude! What about me?"

Before I knew it, Mike had disarticulated one of his legs and thrown it over his shoulder. The exam administrator nearly dropped dead, and I still haven't stopped laughing, ten years later! The people in the room went to pieces, falling around the place, laughing. Before Mike had dismembered himself, you could've cut the tension in the room with a knife. After Mike's antics, everyone was relaxed and ready to face the examination. What a gift he was that day!

Chapter 24

Isn't it interesting, that when God uses our lives and we truly begin to soar, it is easy to gravitate to one of two erroneous extremes? Either we embrace a false humility, failing to recognise and exercise our gifts as fully as we could: or we fall in to the clutches of pride and arrogance so totally, that God no longer uses us in mighty ways. **- Dick Hensley**

Ireland's Call

I was enjoying my time in Philadelphia, but quietly my heart was breaking, as Ireland seemed to be getting further out of reach. It had also been quite some time since my last encounter with my guides, "the voice," or with being called to heal anyone. I seemed to be losing my focus, and in my despair, I was no longer listening. I had developed tunnel vision, and the more upset I became about not being in Ireland, the less I looked for solutions.

I was still doing a good bit of public speaking, and it was at a philosophy event that I embraced one of the most disturbing and powerful lessons I have ever learned in my life. I had prepared what I was going to say; standard material, nothing out of the ordinary. I was speaking last, and while I was waiting in the back of the room, a doctor pulled me aside and showed me an article in some health journal, written by another chiropractor.

The doctor in the editorial was what we would have called a "mixer." A chiropractor that not only adjusted the spine, but used a host of other modalities to treat the symptoms associated with spinal misalignments. The chiropractor that had brought this article to my attention pointed out that this guy thought he was practising *real* chiropractic, but was really just a "wannabe." In a moment of weakness, I let this man's opinions influence me, and when it was my turn to speak, I used the man who had written this piece as a blaring example of what we were fighting against in our profession. At one point, I even think I called him a loser. Before I could make it to the end of the speech, my internal "truth meter" had set off alarm bells and I began to feel physically ill, as I had just compromised my character, my moral standards, and my reputation, to make a guy who was simply "trying a different approach" an embarrassment and an example.

It was me who was embarrassed, in shock at my complete lack of sensitivity. I couldn't even finish the rest of my talk, and promptly announced to the audience that it would be a very long time before they ever heard me speak publicly again. It was that day, that caused me to realise why the last year, and my attempts to get to Ireland, had been such a struggle. I was paddling upstream, against the natural flow of life. I had been such an *expert* in my field, so sure that I knew what was right and true that the philosophy that I thought I had owned, now owned me. That afternoon, I sat in a park, by myself, and wrote a letter of apology to the man I had slandered; *a man I didn't even know*. I made up my mind, then and there; that I would reclaim my power, never allowing apathy or disappointment in my circumstances to dictate my life ever again. I was solid in this decision and I was about to experience just how quickly the Universe responds when we make a real commitment to change.

The very next day, I got a phone call from my dear friend John, asking if it would be possible to give him a hand with opening his new office in Galway, Ireland.

"Ask and ye shall receive." It was so simple, it was scary.

Back on Track

I could hardly wait to get to Ireland, and Dave and I both knew that our relationship had run its course. We finished as friends, remaining that way to this day. When two lives are congruent with their purpose, this is the way that *any* partnership can finish up; with joy, and gratitude for the time shared in each other's lives. Dave took me to the airport, we kissed, and hugged goodbye, not sure when we would see one another again. I was unsure how long I would be in Galway; it could be weeks, or months. There was one thing I was certain of, I would invoke all that I knew to insure, that this time, I was staying in Ireland for good.

The time I spent in Galway was amazing. I learned so much about practicing chiropractic, and what it meant to see a high volume of people. John was in Dublin, so I didn't see him often. That summer, I spent a tremendous amount of time on my own, walking the streets of Galway, sitting at the edge of the sea, so grateful to be on the Irish side of the Atlantic. I was centring my soul, rediscovering my path, and understanding that just because we follow our calling, doesn't mean we are exempt from life's toughest lessons.

When my time in Galway was finished, I still was no closer to finding a way to live permanently in Ireland. I refused to crumble this time, and kept sending out signals to the Universe, that I trusted the process and knew that my prayers would be heard. I got a phone call from my friend Maryellen, in England, inviting me to join her, and some friends, on a sailing trip around the islands of the west coast of Scotland. I could think of nothing I would rather do, so I packed up and flew over to England, where I met up with Maryellen. We drove up to Scotland to meet the rest of the group that would be on the yacht. I was ticking off another lifetime goal, because as much as I loved and longed to be in Ireland, I had always wanted to spend time in the highlands of Scotland. I guess it was because Dad always said he was a descendent of Rob Roy, the famous Scottish warrior, and he had the birthmark to prove it! Both of my parents were of Scottish descent, and I was thrilled to finally get the chance to be there.

The trip around the islands was incredible. The scenery and the wildlife were breathtaking! The experience of being on the crew of this yacht was also a first. The most important part of this trip, however, was the phone call I received two days before we finished the journey. Dr. D, the doc that had come through for me during my externship in Ireland, was about to do it again!

"M.H., when are you back?"

"The day after tomorrow. Why?"

"I have an office I need you to cover. The doctor has gone for good. I need you to stay there until I figure out what I'm going to do."

I could barely speak, but tried not to sound over eager, when in actual fact, I was ready to burst!

"Of course, I can help you out," I said calmly.

"Good," he said. "I'll see you in two days."

"By the way, Dr. D., where is it that I'll be going?"

"The town of Athlone. I'll chat to you later."

I couldn't believe my ears! I was going to be working in the office that I had stopped in a year and a half earlier. This was the office that I had visualised as my own; the one that was located in my very favourite town in Ireland; the one with the secretary with the special gleam in her eye. I screamed to the heavens,

"YOU ROCK!!!"

As clear as day, I heard, "We know, and so do you!"

Just as I knew it would, everything had fallen in to place, and suddenly, there was magic all around me. I had to return back to Philadelphia to pack my belongings. Dave was genuinely happy for me, and never did or said anything that made me feel anything but supported. I would miss him, but now it was my turn to shine!

On the 4th of July, I landed in Dublin, and walked in to arrivals as a resident of Ireland. It gave "Independence Day" a whole new meaning! A new chapter was beginning, and I had no earthly idea what Spirit had in store for me. All I can tell you is that the amazing experiences I had been through in my past would pale in comparison, to what the next ten years had in store.

Initially, it felt as if I had stepped back in time, bringing my expanded understanding of a Universal oneness into a place where separateness appeared to abound, particularly in the case of spirituality and religion. It was 1999, and talk of oppression and fresh memories of the embers of religiously fuelled fires still burned in the hearts of people on both sides of the Irish border. It quickly became clear why I had picked Ireland and why she had picked me. I had barely opened my office doors when people began to arrive, seeking something much deeper than an answer for their physical pain. It was as if they instinctively knew that I could help them to reconnect with a part of themselves that had been overshadowed by fear, guilt and distrust. For me, the fact that I was the student and those who seemingly were seeking my help were to become my teachers was overwhelming. The vast majority of the people I was to interact with had been steeped in religion to the point that they were drowning in it. I was to provide them with the guidance to step beyond the church doors and back in to their own divinity, not turning their back on what they had known but expanding their awareness to reconnect to the God within us all.

My first experience with this was when a prominent citizen of the town walked in to my office on "referral". At first, nothing seemed unusual, as my practice was rapidly building by word of mouth. I was half way through taking a standard medical history when he explained that it was his wife who had told him to come see me. Suddenly, the energy in the room began to shift and this man and I were no longer alone. His wife had sent him to see me alright, but I soon realised that she had been dead for nearly a year. The most incredible story began to unfold as this man told me of his undying love for her. His physical health had declined purely from grief and the first step in his healing process was when his wife appeared to him at a routine morning mass and gave him my name. She went on to tell them that things were very different than they had believed while they grew together as a married couple. She told him that if he went and spoke to me that he would have a better understanding of what she meant. I would venture to guess that the only reason he finally ended up in my office was due to nothing but his love and dedication to this woman, as he admitted that this went against all that he had ever known or believed.

We spent most of the morning reconnecting with his wife, answering questions that had gnawed at his soul concerning the way that she had passed. She answered everything, speaking through me, right down to the fact that she had only appeared to be in distress in the end. Her perceived physical suffering was creating an opportunity for spiritual growth and evolution for her family and friends. In actual fact, she explained in detail how she had mastered the art of detaching her spirit from her body during peak times of pain. Her husband sobbed with relief as she reassured him from another realm. The experience was intense and one that I will never forget as it marked the beginning of my professional career as a facilitator of metaphysical healing.

I love Ireland, as much as I did the first day I set foot on her mystical shores. The bountiful gifts that this country has bestowed on me are so numerous, that I hardly know where to begin. My work as a chiropractor, and healer, has brought such wonder and fulfilment to my life. The opportunity to reconnect that man with his wife was the first of a new series of incredible tales of out of this world encounters. There is also the matter of the circle of twelve; the individuals that the psychic had told me I would meet in the land of the flaming symbols. One by one, these extraordinary beings were finding their way into my life. Each with the same, exact memory and vision of the work we are here to accomplish together. From spiritual councils to communicating with the dead, miracle children to energy orbs; every unique experience to come would mark its place on the circumference of a series of divinely orchestrated *Circles of Light*.

I look forward with great anticipation to sharing the next chapter of my life and express to you my heart felt gratitude for allowing me the opportunity to remind you *who you really are* and that each and every one of us is indeed, *promised*.

Until Next Time…